Contents

Get started in Turkish

Asuman Çelen Pollard

First published in Great Britain in 2003 by Hodder Education. An Hachette UK company.

First published in US in 2003 by The McGraw-Hill Companies, Inc.

This edition published 2014

Copyright © Asuman Çelen Pollard 2003, 2010, 2014

The right of Asuman Çelen Pollard to be identified as the Author of the Work has been asserted by her in accordance with the Copyright, Designs and Patents Act 1988.

Database right Hodder & Stoughton (makers)

The *Teach Yourself* name is a registered trademark of Hachette UK.

British Library Cataloguing in Publication Data: a catalogue record for this title is available from the British Library.

Library of Congress Catalog Card Number: on file.

ISBN 978 1 444 18320 7

10 9 8 7 6 5 4 3 2 1

The publisher has used its best endeavours to ensure that any website addresses referred to in this book are correct and active at the time of going to press. However, the publisher and the author have no responsibility for the websites and can make no guarantee that a site will remain live or that the content will remain relevant, decent or appropriate.

The publisher has made every effort to mark as such all words which it believes to be trademarks. The publisher should also like to make it clear that the presence of a word in the book, whether marked or unmarked, in no way affects its legal status as a trademark.

Every reasonable effort has been made by the publisher to trace the copyright holders of material in this book. Any errors or omissions should be notified in writing to the publisher, who will endeavour to rectify the situation for any reprints and future editions.

Cover photograph © Thinkstock images

Typeset by Integra Software Services Pvt. Ltd., Pondicherry, India.

Printed and bound in Great Britain by CPI Group (UK) Ltd., Croydon, CR0 4YY.

John Murray Learning policy is to use papers that are natural, renewable and recyclable products and made from wood grown in sustainable forests. The logging and manufacturing processes are expected to conform to the environmental regulations of the country of origin.

John Murray Learning

338 Euston Road

London NW1 3BH

www.hodder.co.uk

Also available in ebook and audio

Acknowledgements

For Vanessa-Su Pollard

I would like to say thank you to Nur Kurtoğlu-Hooton for her guidance, continued constructive support and for brightening my days. Your knowledge as an EFL teacher trainer has been invaluable, especially in the modern approaches of learning sections.

Thanks are also due to my student Yasemin Turan for working alongside me, managing emails and keeping me calm throughout the process! I would not have been able to complete the book without her hard-working attitude, creative and linguistic input and meticulous editing skills. Good luck on your budding music career!

Ülkü Gezer and H. Banu Dikel have been my main connection with Turkey – acting as my eyes and ears to keep me updated on the changes in Turkey and the Turkish language. Banu has provided me with excellent authentic translations throughout the book with her beautiful Turkish. Thank you.

I would also like to thank Gurur İbanoğlu for his vast computing skills.

Thank you to my daughter Vanessa for providing me with emotional support and strength.

I would also like to give great thanks to the Hodder & Stoughton management team, especially Morven Dooner, Angela Castro, Sarah Cole and Melissa Baker. Their continued professional contribution and support has been greatly appreciated. Working alongside them has made me realise once more just how much hard work goes into producing a good book.

Last, but by no means least, thank you to Trisha Wick for her great input in the first edition of this book.

Thank you to Aliye Uçar for her thorough work as a proofreader.

About the author

Teaching languages, especially Turkish, is my way of life. I am a linguist, language teacher and writer and have been an enthusiastic researcher of Turkish as a modern language since 1977. I live and work as both a private Turkish language teacher and a Turkish consultant in Birmingham, England. I make regular visits to my homeland, Turkey, when I can.

I have expertise in teaching Turkish both as a foreign language and for specific purposes. Having also taught English as a foreign language, I have a keen interest in undertaking comparative studies between the two languages. I keep up to date with changes that take place within both languages and create materials that are intended to aid learners at all levels, from beginners to advanced.

I am interested in helping learners understand the nuances in lexis and grammar within Turkish through learner-friendly language. To do this, I draw on my many years of classroom experience, which helps me to create materials that respond to a variety of learning needs. These materials can be used in language classes, as well as in one-to-one teaching. They can also be used by the learners themselves as self-study materials.

With my teaching experience and love of all things Turkish and English, I am ideally placed to guide you on your journey through the Turkish language. As I have said elsewhere, 'This book is a chance for me to share some of the things that I believe help people to be a good language learner based on over 30 years of teaching and research experience.' I hope you will have the joy of learning Turkish with the help of this book.

Asuman Çelen Pollard

Introduction

Welcome to *Get started in Turkish*. This course is designed for anyone who wants to acquire the skills to understand, speak and write some basic Turkish to be able to get the most out of a visit to Turkey.

Starting with the alphabet and pronunciation, we have designed the units so that your Turkish builds gradually. We have included topics and situations which visitors to Turkey will find immediately useful. There are ten carefully graded and interlocking units.

We have assumed no previous knowledge of foreign language learning and have avoided grammatical terminology where possible. Since the book is aimed at beginners, we have tried to keep the language points and explanations as simple and straightforward as possible. The Turkish language works very differently from English and some letters of the alphabet look different from English – but do not be put off by this. With some basic knowledge, you will quickly be able to read and speak Turkish. We have focused on Turkish as spoken in Istanbul in the 21st century.

This book is intended for you to use on your own with the support of the accompanying audio, indicated by in your book. It can also be used for studying with a teacher. Each unit contains dialogues which are all recorded and have (natural) English translations at the back of the book, language and culture points with plenty of examples and all the essential vocabulary needed. At the end of each unit there are exercises for practice, including some specific for reading, writing, speaking and listening and **Test yourself**, which is also recorded to allow you to check your progress. At the back of the book you will find the **Answer key** for the exercises, a **Turkish–English glossary**, an **Appendix of Vowel Harmony** and a **Grammar index**.

How this book works

As modern Turkish is a phonetic language, the Turkish alphabet and pronunciation is introduced in the first section. Take a look at the letters, listen to them more than once, then imitate the sounds you hear. Once you have practised, you can refer back to this section if you need to. There are many more sections in the book which will allow you to practise your pronunciation. Unit 3 concentrates more so on the alphabet and examples of Turkish names to allow you to practise further.

All units open with a cultural reading in English and a **Vocabulary builder** page with accompanying audio. You will often notice missing words in the **Vocabulary builder**. Look for patterns within the readings to help you complete the list for yourself. Each unit has at least two dialogues. Most of the dialogues have very simple gist and comprehension questions before and after. You can choose whether you read or listen to each dialogue first. Whichever way you decide, listen to and read the dialogues a number of times before answering the questions that follow. Answer the questions and check them in the **Answer key** at the back of the book. Be sure to read the **Language discovery** and **Go further** points carefully and then go back to the dialogue. The **Language discovery** section asks you to think about one or more aspects of the grammar seen in the dialogues. (See **Learn to learn** for more about the learning approach, the **Discovery method**, used in this book.)

Don't worry if you don't understand everything straight away; your understanding will improve as time goes on. Don't try to learn all of the items in the vocabulary lists off by heart – you can always go back at any time. Remember, in real life people do not learn lists of vocabulary by rote – they are exposed to words over and over again in a familiar context, and in the end (with a little looking-up or asking) it sticks.

Speak along with the dialogues as you get to know them and imitate what you hear. Don't be afraid to make mistakes; after all, making mistakes is a part of your learning process.

The **Practice**, **Listening**, **Speaking**, and **Reading and writing** exercises are where you can have some fun. If you want to write the answers in the book, do so in pencil. Then you can rub them out later and try again. Don't try an exercise until you are pretty sure you have understood everything that precedes it. When you have completed a couple of units, go back to the exercises in earlier units – it is very satisfying to find them easier to do than the first time!

A complete **Answer key** appears at the end of the book. A glossary of Turkish–English words is provided at the end of the book, as well as an **Appendix of vowel harmony** and a **Grammar index**.

Set yourself a routine for learning, somewhere relaxed. Look at the **Learn to learn** section at the front of the book. You will find the advice helpful, especially if you are returning to learning after a long break.

To make your learning easier and more efficient, a system of icons indicates the actions you should take and the type of activity:

Play the audio

New words and phrases

Listen and pronounce

Figure something out for yourself

Culture and language tips

Exercises

Speak Turkish out loud

Reading

Writing

Check your Turkish

Learn to learn

The Discovery method/Inductive approach

Why use the Discovery method?

▶ It moves the focus away from the traditional teaching method of given knowledge to discovering knowledge for yourself.

▶ It moves the focus away from set rules to everyday use – and use is, after all, the aim in language learning.

▶ It encourages learner autonomy. If learners can find out rules for themselves, then they are making significant steps towards being independent. We can take this further by letting learners decide what aspect of the language in a text they want to analyse.

▶ It teaches a very important skill – how to use real/almost real language to find out the specific language rules. This approach encourages an independent learning style, which stimulates and motivates learners.

▶ It can be particularly effective with low levels and with certain types of learners. It enables these students to focus on use, rather than complex rules and terminology.

▶ If we use authentic material as our context, then learners are in contact with real language, not course-book language.

▶ The rules and structures learners discover are often more valid, relevant and authentic than in a deductive approach, as they can be drawn from real use of the language.

▶ The action of discovery helps learners remember.

▶ This process allows the learner to be in contact with and use the language, then to be able to find rules and apply them to new contexts.

▶ We can support and encourage new learning styles and strategies for all language learners to find rules and examples and improve their learning skills.

The Discovery method – Learn to learn!

There are lots of philosophies and approaches to language learning, some practical, some quite unconventional, and far too many to list here. Perhaps you know of a few, or even have some techniques of your own. In this book we have incorporated the **Discovery method** of learning, a sort of DIY approach to language learning. What this means is that you will be encouraged throughout the course to engage your mind and figure out the language for yourself, through identifying patterns, understanding grammar concepts, noticing words that are similar to English and more. This method promotes **language awareness**, a critical skill in acquiring a new language. As a result of your own efforts, you will be able to better retain what you have learned, use it with confidence and, even better, apply those same skills to continuing to learn the language (or, indeed, another one) on your own after you've finished this book. If you wish to continue learning Turkish, why not try *Complete Turkish*?

Everyone can succeed in learning a language – the key is to know how to learn it. Learning is more than just reading or memorizing grammar and vocabulary. It's about being an **active** learner, learning in real contexts and, most importantly, using what you've learned in different situations. Simply put, if you **figure something out for yourself**, you're more likely to understand it.

And because many of the essential but (let's admit it!) dull details, such as grammar rules, are introduced through the **Discovery method**, you'll have more fun while learning. Soon, the language will start to make sense and you'll be relying on your own intuition to construct original sentences independently, not just listening and repeating.

Enjoy yourself!

WHAT KIND OF LEARNER ARE YOU?

▶ **The visual learner** might benefit from writing down words and phrases over and over again.
▶ **The auditory learner** could gain from reading out loud or recording his/her own vocabulary and listening back.
▶ **The kinaesthetic learner** may enjoy learning in a group or using flashcards, pictures or anything else that satisfies the need to 'experience'.
▶ A mixture of two or more.

Be sure not to limit yourself to one method; try all three and see what works best for you.

This book is for all kinds of people learning Turkish, for a wide range of reasons. This may be the first time you have tried to learn another language. We have planned the units to build up your Turkish gradually, step by step – but once you have started, you may want to explore the book at your own pace. One of the advantages of a self-study book like this is that you can return to a section as many times as you need, working at your own speed.

Here are some tips on language learning that you may find helpful in getting the most out of this book:

1 Be active in your learning. Find out which ways of learning work for you. Everyone is different.

2 Do a little bit every day. Don't expect to be able to learn large amounts in one sitting. Set yourself a goal of learning a certain number of new words every day, say 5–10.

3 Create learning habits. Set time aside for your learning on a regular basis. Stick to a routine.

4 Don't wait till you can speak the language perfectly. Talk to yourself!

5 Be positive about your achievements. Enjoy learning. Concentrate on what you have learned, not on what you cannot remember.

6 Get a good dictionary. When you come across a new word, try to guess the meaning first, then use a good dictionary to check. If you want to learn the word, write it down, with the definition and the word in context.

7 Create your own personal vocabulary book. Group the words either in grammar type (e.g., separate sections for verbs, nouns and adjectives), or by theme (e.g., food, drink, transport, numbers), or according to the purpose they serve in conversation (e.g., how to greet people/how to shop/how to order a meal).

8 Don't worry too much about making mistakes. Mistakes are a natural part of learning. Turkish speakers will be pleased that you are having a go and will appreciate anything you can say.

9 Revise regularly. Use the audio to help you practise speaking and listening, and answer the questions at the end of each unit.

10 Forgetting and relearning is all part of the process. Remember the 5 Rs – Recognise, Revise, Recap, Repeat and Reinforce.

11   Listen carefully. Listen to the audio or, if possible, a native speaker or a teacher, repeating out loud whenever possible. Talk to yourself.

12   Record yourself and compare your pronunciation with a native speaker who speaks standard Turkish, then try again.

13   Make flashcards. Write the Turkish words you are trying to learn on small cards and stick them around the house where you will come across them during the day. Relevant pictures could be an extra support for word meanings.

14   Don't give up. Keep going, using little treats or rewards for your achievements along the way to keep up your motivation. Enjoy it.

The alphabet and pronunciation

The Latin alphabet was adopted by the Republic of Turkey in 1928. Prior to that, Turkish was written in Arabic script. Nowadays, Turkish uses the Latin script, with a small number of modifications. It has 29 letters: eight of them (**a**, **ı**, **o**, **u**, **e**, **i**, **ö**, **ü**) are vowels, the remaining 21 are consonants. Some vowels differ from English sounds, but English speakers can pronounce all of the sounds with little difficulty. Once you have learned the alphabet, you will find Turkish simple and straightforward to read, because unlike English:

▶ you pronounce Turkish in exactly the same way as you spell it.
▶ each Turkish letter stands for a single sound.

Here is the Turkish alphabet. This book focuses on Turkish as spoken in Istanbul at the turn of the 21st century, which is Standard Turkish.

 00.01 **Listen to the alphabet while looking at the following list of sounds, then repeat the sounds out loud as you hear them.**

Turkish letter	Approximate letter name in English	Approximate English sound
Aa	ah	*art*
Bb	bay	*big*
Cc	jay	*John*
Çç	chay	*child*
Dd	dey	*do*
Ee	ey	*get*
Ff	fey	*far*
Gg	gay	*get*
Ğğ yumuşak ğ	yumushak *gay*	(This letter has no sound!)
Hh	hey	*how*
Iı	uh	*butter*
İi	ee	*it*

Jj	zhe	*pleasure*
Kk	kay	*kitten*
Ll	ley	*lovely*
Mm	mey	*man*
Nn	ney	*no*
Oo	o	*box*
Öö	ur	*dirt*
Pp	pay	*pen*
Rr	ray	*dry*
Ss	say	*sea*
Şş	shay	*show*
Tt	tay	*tea*
Uu	oo	*pull*
Üü	ew	*German ü or French tu*
Vv	vey	*very*
Yy	ye	*yes*
Zz	zey	*zip*

Note the difference between **İ** or **i** with a dot and **I** or **ı** without a dot.

In English we do not always pronounce every letter. Turkish is different – you always pronounce all the letters. What you see is what you say! The only slight exception is the letter **ğ**. The letter **ğ** is called **yumuşak g**, which means *soft g*. It always comes after a vowel and turns that vowel into a long sound. You might think of it as doubling the vowel before it. Therefore, think of **ağ** as *aa* or think of **öğle** as *ööle*. There are no words beginning with *soft g* (**ğ**).

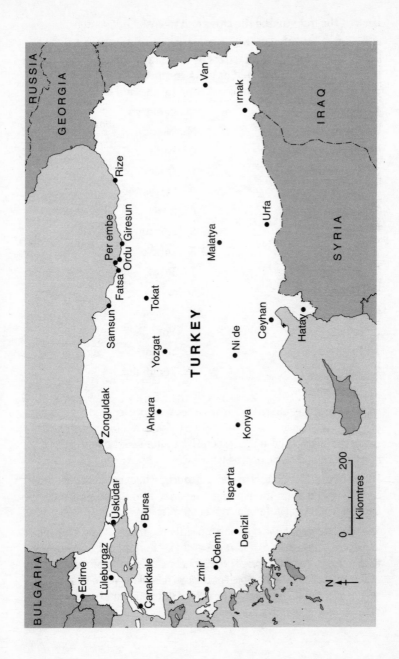

Look at the map to find the cities and towns!

 00.02 **And now it's your turn to practise, starting with A for Ankara. Listen to the following 29 letters of the Turkish alphabet and repeat the example words out loud as you hear them. They are all towns and cities in Turkey, except one. Listen for the odd one out!**

A	Ankara	M	Malatya
B	Bursa	N	Niğde
C	Ceyhan	O	Ordu
Ç	Çanakkale	Ö	Ödemiş
D	Denizli	P	Perşembe
E	Edirne	R	Rize
F	Fatsa	S	Samsun
G	Giresun	Ş	Şırnak
Ğ	yumuşak G	T	Tokat
H	Hatay	U	Urfa
I	Isparta	Ü	Üsküdar
İ	İzmir	V	Van
J	Japonya	Y	Yozgat
K	Konya	Z	Zonguldak
L	Lüleburgaz		

For more practice turn to Unit 3. Now that you have learned the sounds of Turkish you can read a newspaper even if you cannot understand it! But at this stage, knowing your sounds and letters will be very useful if you need to look at a menu or phrase book.

Pronunciation is important in relaying exactly what you mean. Getting certain aspects of the pronunciation wrong could mean the difference between ending up in Torquay rather than Turkey!

The small matter of two dots above a letter can make a large difference in meaning. Take **Kurt** and **Kürt**, for example. **Kurt** means *wolf*; however, **Kürt** refers to *Kurdish people*. The slight difference in the pronunciation of **u** and **ü** will determine which of the two meanings you are referring to. It is important, therefore, to be able to distinguish and produce the differences in sound that each letter makes.

ACCENT

Accents are difficult to get right in any language – even your own! You should not worry too much about acquiring the perfect Turkish accent. An accent good enough to be understood will do for most purposes. If you have the choice, do try to imitate the standard accent – Istanbul pronunciation – so you will be understood wherever you go!

STRESS

Turkish words carry only a very light stress, generally on the last syllable. On the whole, compared to English, stresses are hardly noticeable. As a general rule of thumb, you should try to stress the last syllable of a word (lightly).

RHYTHM

When we listen to someone speak, we do not just listen to and try to hear the individual words to understand the meaning; we also listen to the rhythm of the speech.

Turkish rhythm is different from English rhythm. If you use English rhythm when you speak Turkish, your listeners will find it difficult to understand you. This can happen even if you pronounce each syllable of each word correctly. Rhythm is not something that is easy to get right through conscious effort. You need exposure to it. The best way of getting the rhythm is to listen, listen, listen and copy, copy, copy. You can listen to the audio accompanying this book and Turkish television or radio via satellite or on the internet.

Do not worry about making mistakes. Everyone makes mistakes, and they are an integral and important part of learning.

Bol şanslar! *Enjoy learning Turkish!*

Survival guide – useful expressions

As well as introducing you to Turkish pronunciation, this section will give you a kick-start in survival words and phrases. Listen to the items listed while looking at how they are spelled. Repeat the words out loud as you hear them.

BASICS

00.04

evet	*yes*
hayır	*no*
lütfen	*please*
mersi	*thanks*
sağ olun	*thank you*
merhaba/selam	*hello*
hoşça kalın	*goodbye*
Nasılsınız?	*How are you?*
iyiyim	*I'm fine*
pardon	*sorry, excuse me*

TALKING

Anladım.	*I understand.*
Anlamadım.	*I don't understand.*
hızlı	*fast*
tekrar	*again*
yavaş	*slowly*
Ne demek?	*What does it mean?*
İngilizce	*English*
Türkçesi ne?	*What is it in Turkish?*

SHOPPING

00.05

Kaç lira?	*How much (money)?*
ucuz	*cheap*
pahalı	*expensive*
var	*there is some*
yok	*there isn't any*
pul	*stamp*
jeton	*token* (formerly used in public telephones; now used for public transport)
pazar	*market*

EATING

00.06

restoran/lokanta	*restaurant*
bakar mısınız!	*waiter! excuse me!*
fiyat listesi	*price list*
mönü	*menu*
hesap	*bill*
öğle yemeği	*lunch*
akşam yemeği	*dinner*

DIRECTIONS

00.07

Nerede?	*Where?*
sol	*left*
sağ	*right*
düz	*straight on*
Kaç kilometre?	*How many kilometres?*
yavaş	*slow/slowly*
dur	*stop*

TRAVELLING

00.08

Ne zaman?	*When?*
Hangi otobüs?	*Which bus?*
ilk	*first*
son	*last*
bilet	*ticket*
burada	*here*
İnecek var.	*I want to get out/off.*
Ne kadar sürer?	*How long does it take?*

ACCOMMODATION

00.09

bir kişi	*one person*
bir gece	*one night*
sıcak su	*hot water*
devamlı su	*non-stop water*
kahvaltı dahil	*breakfast included*
Gecesi kaç lira?	*How much is a night?*

TIMES

00.10

dakika	*minute*
saat	*hour*
hafta	*week*
şimdi	*now*
sonra	*later*
gün	*day*
dün	*yesterday*
bugün	*today*
yarın	*tomorrow*
önce	*earlier/ago*
sonra	*then/later*

QUANTITIES AND NUMBERS

00.11

az	*little*
çok	*a lot*
sıfır	*zero*
bir	*one*
iki	*two*
üç	*three*
dört	*four*
beş	*five*
yüz	*hundred*
bin	*thousand*
milyon	*million*
milyar	*billion*

PLACES

00.12

tuvalet	*toilet*
postane	*post office*
eczane	*chemist's*
otogar	*bus station*
iskele	*jetty, ferry stop*
bakkal	*grocer's shop*
havaalanı	*airport*
karakol	*police station*

QUESTION WORDS

00.13

Hangi?	*Which?*
Ne?	*What?*
Ne kadar?	*How much?*
Ne zaman?	*When?*
Var mı?	*Is there?/Have you got?*

Nasıl?	*How?*
Nasılsınız?	*How are you?*
Nerede?	*Where?*
Nereli?	*Where from?*
Kaç kişi?	*How many people?*
Kim?	*Who?*
Kimin?	*Whose?*
Kaç günlük?	*How many days?*
Kaç tane?	*How many?*
Kaça?	*How much?*
Neden/Niçin?	*Why?*

TROUBLE

00.14

İmdat!	*Help!*
kaza	*accident*
doktor	*doctor*
Çok ayıp!	*Shame on you!* (use this to repel unwanted advances)
ambulans	*ambulance*

LANGUAGE

Ne demek?	*What does it mean?*
Nasıl yazılır?	*How do you spell it?*
Nasıl denir?	*How do you say/pronounce it?*
Pardon?	*Excuse me?*
Daha yavaş, lütfen.	*More slowly, please.*

1 Selamlaşma
Greetings

In this unit you will learn how to:
▶ *greet people, say goodbye and introduce yourself.*
▶ *use the expressions for Mr, Mrs, Ms, Miss.*
▶ *use the numbers 0–10.*
▶ *use the formal and informal words for you.*

CEFR: *(A1) Can establish basic social contact by using the simplest everyday polite forms of: greetings and farewells; introductions; saying please, thank you and sorry.*

Greeting people in Turkey

Türkiye'de (*In Turkey*), social kissing on both cheeks is common between people of the same sex. Young, Westernised **Türkler** (*Turks*) shake hands when greeting each other and kiss on both cheeks. Strict **Müslümanlar** (*Muslims*) do not kiss or shake hands with the opposite sex, only with the same sex. Kissing in public between opposite genders is not socially acceptable. Kissing an elderly or higher status person's hand is a way of showing respect and is common practice.

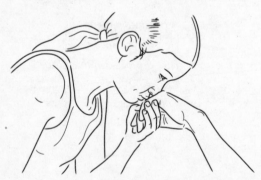

Generally, many **İngilizler** (*English people*) are more concerned with maintaining their personal space than **Türkler**, who often express themselves through physical contact. **İngilizler** are considered to be more reserved than **Türkler**, who will often express their emotions quite openly.

The collective words for Turks and Muslims are given, but how would you say:

1 one Turkish person
2 one Muslim person

 # Vocabulary builder

SELAMLAŞMA *GREETINGS*

 01.01 Listen and repeat. Then complete the missing parts of the Turkish expressions.

Günaydın.	*Good morning.*
İyi akşamlar.	*Good evening.*
_____ geceler.	*Good night.*
Merhaba./Selam.	*Hello./Hi.*
_____ günler.	*Have a good day.*

HANGİ SAATLERDE *TIMES OF THE DAY*

 01.02 **Listen and repeat. Then answer the questions.**

Günaydın
(7 a.m. to midday)

Merhaba/Selam
(afternoon)

İyi akşamlar
(5–10 p.m.)

İyi geceler
(after 10 p.m.)

İyi günler
(all day)

a How would you greet someone at 10 a.m.?
b How would you greet someone at 8 p.m.?

NEW EXPRESSIONS

Listen to the words and phrases you will hear in the dialogues. Practise listening and saying the expressions until you feel you have learned them.

Dialogue 1 Good evening

01.03

ben	*I*
Ya siz?	*And you?* (singular formal)
Nasılsınız?	*How are you?* (formal)
Hanım	*Miss/Ms/Mrs* (formal; placed after the first name)
teşekkürler	*thanks*
Bey	*Mr* (formal; placed after the first name)
İyiyim.	*I am fine.*
siz/sen	*you*
ben de	*me too* (lit. *I too*)
şarap	*wine*
evet/hayır	*yes/no*
lütfen	*please*

Dialogue 2 Hi! How are you?

01.04

Nasılsın?	*How are you?* (informal)
sen	*you* (singular; for emphasis in response to **nasılsın?**)
bira	*beer*

Dialogue 3 It's a very nice party

01.05

Ya sen?	*And you?* (singular informal)
çok	*very*
güzel	*beautiful, nice, great*
bir	*one* (can be used to mean *a* or *an*)
parti	*party*
değil	*not*
değil mi?	*isn't it?*

Dialogue 4 Goodbye

 01.06

hoşça kalın	*goodbye* (formal)
güle güle	*goodbye* (response to **hoşça kalın**)

Dialogues

Read the introduction and the gist question for each conversation. Then listen or read the conversation and answer the questions.

1 GOOD EVENING

 01.07 *Ülkü, Doktor Bahadır Bey, Hüseyin and Banu are all at a party in a club. Ülkü is married to Bahadır, who joins them later. He is in his forties. Hüseyin approaches Ülkü and introduces himself.*

1 How do you know it is evening?

Hüseyin	İyi akşamlar, ben Hüseyin. Ya, siz?
Ülkü	İyi akşamlar, ben Ülkü.
Hüseyin	Nasılsınız, Ülkü Hanım?
Ülkü	Teşekkürler, Hüseyin Bey. İyiyim. Siz nasılsınız?
Hüseyin	Ben de iyiyim.
(They shake hands. Hüseyin offers Ülkü a glass of wine.)	
Hüseyin	Şarap?
Ülkü	Evet, lütfen.

2 What does Ülkü accept?

2 HI! HOW ARE YOU?

 01.08 *Then Ülkü's husband joins them.*

1 Are the speakers using formal or informal greetings?

Bahadır	Merhaba Ülkü, nasılsın?
Ülkü	İyiyim, teşekkürler. Sen nasılsın?
Bahadır	Ben de iyiyim.

(They kiss each other on both cheeks. Ülkü offers Bahadır a beer.)

Ülkü	Bira?
Bahadır	Evet, lütfen.

2 Does Bahadır want a beer?

3 IT'S A VERY NICE PARTY

 01.09 *Ülkü introduces herself to Banu, who is 30 years old. Later on, Bahadır joins the conversation.*

1 Who is enjoying the party?

Ülkü	İyi akşamlar, ben Ülkü. Ya, sen?
Banu	İyi akşamlar, ben Banu.

(They shake hands.)

Ülkü	Nasılsın, Banu?
Banu	Teşekkürler, iyiyim.
Ülkü	Çok güzel bir parti, değil mi?
Banu	Evet, çok güzel.
Ülkü	Banu, Dr Bahadır Bey.

2 Which phrase means *very nice*?

3 How do you know Dr Bahadır is a man?

4 GOODBYE

01.10 *Bahadır joins the group.*

1 How do you know Banu is being polite and respectful with Bahadır?

Bahadır	İyi akşamlar.
Banu	İyi akşamlar, Bahadır Bey.
Bahadır	Nasılsın, Banu?
Banu	Teşekkürler, iyiyim. Siz nasılsınız?
Bahadır	Ben de iyiyim.
(Banu looks at her watch.)	
Banu	Hoşça kalın, Ülkü Hanım. Hoşça kalın, Bahadır Bey. İyi geceler.
Ülkü and Bahadır	Güle güle, Banu.

2 How is Banu?

3 How does Banu say goodbye?

Language discovery

1 Answer these questions about the dialogues. Use Turkish where possible.
   a How does Hüseyin say *good evening*?
   b Name two beverages at the party.
   c What does Banu say to agree that it is a good party?
   d How does Ülkü say goodbye to Banu?

2 Practise the dialogues, using your name and the names of people you know.

3 Match the questions and answers.

a	İyi akşamlar.	**1**	Merhaba
b	Nasılsınız?	**2**	Evet, lütfen.
c	Şarap?	**3**	Teşekkürler. İyiyim. Siz nasılsınız?
d	Merhaba.	**4**	İyiyim. Teşekkürler. Sen nasılsın?
e	Nasılsın?	**5**	İyi akşamlar.

4 Find the two phrases below in Dialogues 1 and 2. Which endings follow each, *-sın* or *-sınız*? Notice how Ülkü uses one form with someone she's just met and another form with her husband.

   a Siz nasıl _____?

   b Sen nasıl _____?

5 Put the following words in order to make questions with *değil mi?* and *bir.*

   a mi? güzel, Çay değil

   _____

   b mi? Güzel çay, bir değil

   _____

   c bir değil parti, güzel mi? Çok

   _____

Go further

1 USING *SEN* OR *SİZ* (*YOU*)

You probably noticed that Ülkü changed the form of her language slightly in each conversation, although she meant the same thing.

Turkish has two ways of saying *you*, depending on how well you know the other person. **Sen** means you are speaking to a person you know well. So in the second part of the conversation Ülkü asked her husband, **Sen nasılsın?**

 Name three people you would use *Sen nasılsın?* with.

If you are speaking to a person you do not know, use **siz** for *you*. You also use **siz** to show respect to someone who is older or of a higher social standing, such as your boss. So when meeting Hüseyin for the first time Ülkü asked **Siz nasılsınız?** (Remember, when you use **siz**, **nasılsın** changes to **nasılsınız?**) If you use **siz** when speaking to someone, they will think you are polite and respectful – so if in doubt, use **siz**!

 Name three people you would use *Siz nasılsınız?* with.

Siz also always means *you* when you are speaking to more than one person, even if you know them very well.

Nasıl?	*How is he/she/it?*
Sen nasılsın?	*How are you?* (informal)
Siz nasılsınız?	*How are you?* (formal and plural form)

Remember to use the formal **siz** when addressing:
- ▶ someone you don't know
- ▶ someone who is older than you
- ▶ someone to whom you want to show respect
- ▶ more than one person.

Use the informal **sen** when:
- ▶ talking to a friend
- ▶ you use first names
- ▶ you speak to a younger person.

If you are familiar with languages like French or Spanish, you'll notice that **sen** and **siz** function like *tu/vous* or *tú/Ud.*

2 *HANIM* AND *BEY* WITH NAMES

Türkiye'de (In Turkey) surnames are not used when greeting people. If you want to be polite, you use the person's first name with **Hanım** (for a woman) and **Bey** (for a man). Ülkü and Hüseyin are being courteous on first meeting, so Ülkü said **Teşekkürler Hüseyin Bey** and Hüseyin referred to her as **Ülkü Hanım**. First names are used without **Hanım** or **Bey**, as in **Teşekkürler, Hüseyin Bey**, only if you know the person well and you are roughly the same age.

3 WORDS THAT ARE BORROWED FROM OTHER LANGUAGES

Turkish belongs to a different family of languages. However, there are many words similar to English. Turkish has a lot of words that are borrowed from English and others that are borrowed or derived from Arabic, Persian, French, German and Latin. **Bravo** is a word that you will hear often in Turkey. **Parti** is an example of a word in this unit that is borrowed from English. Another word you might recognise is **tuvalet** for *toilet*.

4 *BİR*

In Turkish, there is no word that means *a/an* or *the*. Sometimes **bir**, which means *one*, is used to mean *a* or *an*.

bir parti   *a party*

5 DEĞİL

To make a word or phrase negative (e.g., *It's not . . .*), place **değil** after the word or phrase.

Bira değil.	*Not beer.*
Şarap değil.	*Not wine.*
Parti değil.	*Not a party.*

Değil mi changes a word or a phrase into the question *isn't it?* or *aren't they?* Look at the following examples:

Şarap, değil mi?	*It's wine, isn't it?*
Çok güzel bir parti, değil mi?	*It's a very good party, isn't it?*

Practice

1 Reorder the sentences to make a dialogue between two friends. The first one is done for you. Also underline the ending used after *sen*.

a Hoşça kal. ___
b İyiyim, sen nasılsın? ___
c Merhaba Gülen, nasılsın? ___
d Ben de iyiyim. ___
e Merhaba, Ali. _1_
f Güle güle. ___

2 Read the sentences and answer the questions.

a Teşekkürler, Hüseyin Bey.
How do you know Hüseyin is a man? _____
b Nasılsınız Ülkü Hanım?
How do you know Ülkü is a woman? _____

3 Match the Turkish words with their English equivalents.

a	parti	**1**	toilet
b	tuvalet	**2**	bravo
c	bravo	**3**	email
d	posta	**4**	party

4 What does *bir* mean in the following sentences?

a Çok güzel bir parti.
b Çok güzel bir bira.
c Çok güzel bir şarap.

5 **Fill in the blanks with *değil* or *değil mi*.**
   a Bira _____.
   b Şarap, _____?
   c Parti çok güzel _____.
   d Parti çok güzel, _____?
   e Hüseyin Hanım _____.
   f Banu güzel, _____?

6 **Fill in the blanks with *değil* or *değil mi*. Add ? or . at the end of sentences.**
   a Bira _____
      Bira _____, şarap lütfen. Teşekkürler.
   b Parti çok güzel, _____
      Evet çok güzel.
   c Deniz Bey, _____ Ben Elizabeth.
      Memnun oldum*, Elizabeth Hanım.

* **Memnun oldum.** = *Glad to meet you.*

🎙 Pronunciation

LETTERS

01.11 When the letter **ğ** comes after a vowel, it turns that vowel into a long sound. You might think of **ğ** as doubling the vowel before it. So **değil** is pronounced as **deeil**. In colloquial Turkish you will often hear **diil**. Listen and repeat these expressions.

Bira değil.

Şarap değil.

Parti değil.

NUMBERS 0–10

1 01.12 **Listen, read and repeat.**

0	sıfır	6	altı
1	bir	7	yedi
2	iki	8	sekiz
3	üç	9	dokuz
4	dört	10	on
5	beş		

2 Complete the table with the correct word or number. Then cover the bottom row and test yourself.

0	1		3		5		7		9	
	bir	iki		dört		altı		sekiz		on

 00 = TUVALET

In Turkey, you might see 00 on a door. It simply means *toilet*! Knowing this may just come in very handy when you are in Turkey.

Tuvalet nerede?   *Where is the toilet?*

Listening

01.13 **Listen to Dialogues 1 and 2 again. Look at the *parti* picture and identify the people.**

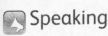

Speaking

01.14 Role play. Listen to the conversation. Then practice role playing each part.

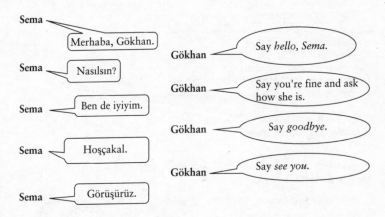

Sema — Merhaba, Gökhan.

Gökhan — Say *hello, Sema.*

Sema — Nasılsın?

Gökhan — Say you're fine and ask how she is.

Sema — Ben de iyiyim.

Gökhan — Say *goodbye.*

Sema — Hoşçakal.

Gökhan — Say *see you.*

Sema — Görüşürüz.

Reading and writing

1 Read the email and answer the questions.

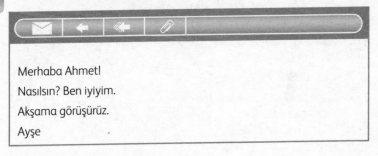

Merhaba Ahmet!

Nasılsın? Ben iyiyim.

Akşama görüşürüz.

Ayşe

   a Who is the **e-posta** from?
   b Who is it to?
   c When are they meeting?

2 Now write a similar email to a friend in Turkey. Use the email in Question 1 as a model.

Nslsn   is short for **Nasılsın**.

Mrb   is short for **Merhaba**.

Grsz   is short for **Görüşürüz**.

Kib is short for **Kendine iyi bak**.

3 Look at the message and answer the questions.

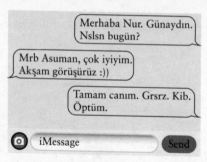

> Merhaba Nur. Günaydın. Nslsn bugün?

> Mrb Asuman, çok iyiyim. Akşam görüşürüz :))

> Tamam canım. Grsrz. Kib. Öptüm.

iMessage   Send

a Is it morning or evening?
b When will they meet?

? Test yourself

1 How would you say hello to the following people at the time shown? More than one answer is possible.

  a To your friends   **c** To your boss
  b To your grandmother

2 It is late at night and you decide to go to bed. What would you say to your Turkish friends?

3 How would you say goodbye to your Turkish host?

4 What would the response be?

5 Fill in the blanks to complete the greeting and introduction below.

  a M _____, ben Şafak.
  b Selam, _____ Gökhan.

6 Write the correct English word for each number.

a beş	**d** dokuz	**g** dört	**j** sekiz
b on	**e** üç	**h** iki	**k** sıfır
c bir	**f** yedi	**i** altı	

7 Add or subtract these numbers. Write the answers in digits.

a dört + üç = _____ **f** dört – iki = _____

b bir + bir = _____ **g** beş – iki = _____

c _____ + üç = dört **h** _____ – bir = dokuz

d dört + _____ = dokuz **i** dokuz – _____ = sekiz

e iki + altı = _____

8 Look at the word search. There are ten words which you have learned. Can you find them and write them down? One has been found for you.

M	E	R	H	A	B	A	B	İ	R
N	R	S	A	V	E	Z	A	K	T
A	C	İ	N	O	Y	D	O	İ	R
S	L	A	I	N	P	J	S	T	V
I	R	C	M	P	O	U	S	E	N
L	F	N	O	P	Z	H	İ	B	J
S	A	L	T	İ	R	S	Z	J	C
I	B	N	T	R	P	S	O	V	J
N	İ	Y	İ	Y	İ	M	R	T	U
P	S	I	R	G	D	Ç	F	O	N

9 01.15 **Listen and answer the following questions orally or in writing.**

a How do you say *hello*?

b How do you say *goodbye*?

c How do you say *goodnight*?

d How do you ask your boss how she is?

e How do you ask your friend how he is?

If you get any wrong, go back through the unit and have another look before moving on to the next unit.

SELF CHECK

I CAN...
. . . greet people, say goodbye and introduce myself.
. . . use the expressions for *Mr, Mrs, Ms, Miss*.
. . . use the numbers 0–10.
. . . use the formal and informal words for *you*.

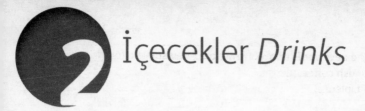

2 İçecekler *Drinks*

In this unit you will learn how to:

▶ *order drinks and snacks.*
▶ *ask for a menu or the bill.*
▶ *use the numbers 10–100.*
▶ *say basic colours.*

CEFR: *(A1) Can order drinks, snacks and bar food, ask for a menu and the bill and leave a tip for the waiter.*

Having a drink in Turkey

In Turkey all the usual European drinks are available, including soft drinks, spirits, beer, wine, mineral water and fruit juices. However, you'll want to try some typical Turkish drinks such as **rakı** (*a strong aniseed spirit usually diluted with water*), **vişne suyu** (*sour cherry juice*), **ayran** (*a yogurt drink*), **çay** (*tea*) and **Türk kahvesi** (*Turkish coffee*). **Çay** is served black in a tulip-shaped glass, usually with sugar cubes placed on the saucer. The colour of the tea is all-important, as it is a guide to its quality. **Türk kahvesi** is also served black but in a small china cup, slightly smaller than an espresso cup. Sugar, if desired, is added when the coffee is being made, so you will need to learn the words to order coffee *with sugar* (**şekerli**), *without sugar* (**sade**) or *with a little sugar* (**az şekerli**). The coffee and sugar are heated in a **cezve** (*a small pot with a long handle*). If you want instant coffee, you need to ask for **Nescafé***. The preparation of both tea and coffee are real art forms. Turks say that offering a cup of Turkish coffee invites 40 years of friendship.

*In Turkey, any instant coffee is called Nescafé even though this is the name of a product.

> **TIP**
>
> **Rakı**, when mixed with water, turns white and is known as **arslan sütü** *lion's milk* because of its strength and colour. When **rakı** is ordered in a bar, it is usually served with **beyaz peynir** *white cheese*, **zeytin** *olives* and **fıstık** *nuts*.

Look for the new words above. How would you say the following?
1 One Turkish coffee, please.
2 One tea, please.

Vocabulary builder

A GLASS OF TEA, PLEASE

 02.01 **Listen and repeat. Then complete the missing parts of the Turkish expressions.**

Bir _____ çay, lütfen.	*A glass of tea, please.*
Bir _____ çay.	*A glass of tea.*

NEW EXPRESSIONS

Listen to the words and phrases you will hear in the dialogues. Practise listening and saying the expressions until you feel you have learned them.

Dialogue 1 A glass of tea, please

 02.02

Buyrun[1], efendim?	*How can I help you, sir/madam?*
şişe	*bottle*
yok	*there is none/we haven't got any*
içecek	*drink*
ne	*what*
var	*there is/are*
mönü	*menu*
teşekkür	*thank you* (alternative to **teşekkürler**)
Nescafé	*instant coffee*
süt	*milk*
sütlü	*with milk*
tamam	*OK*
şeker	*sugar*
Afiyet olsun.	*Enjoy your drinks!/Enjoy your meal!*
garson[2]	*waiter/waitress*
buyrun	*yes, sir*
hesap	*the bill*
üstü kalsın	*keep the change*
sağ olun	*thanks* (showing respect and gratitude)

[1] **Buyurun** is the correct dictionary spelling. **Buyrun** is what people say.

[2] **Garson** is borrowed from French; it means either *waiter* or *waitress*.

Dialogue 2 The coffee is very good here

 02.03

şekerli	*sweet*
bana da	*for me too*
şekersiz	*plain, without sugar*
yavrum	*my child (shows affection)*
limonata	*traditional lemonade*
ayran	*ayran (yogurt-based drink)*
sade	*without sugar*
içecekleriniz	*your drinks*
afiyet olsun	*enjoy your drinks*
Acıktım.	*I'm hungry.*
tost	*toasted sandwich*
peynirli tost	*toasted cheese sandwich*
manzara	*view*

TIP

The ending **-lı** means *with*, and **-sız** means *without*. (See Unit 6 for grammar explanations.)

Dialogue 3 One red wine, please

 02.04

şarap	*wine*
kırmızı	*red*
kırmızı mı?	*red? (See Unit 4 for explanation of **mı?**)*
beyaz	*white*
beyaz mı?	*white?*
ve	*and*
çerez	*snacks*
fıstık	*nuts*
biraz da	*and (some) also*
karışık	*mixed*
meyve	*fruit*
peynir	*cheese*

Dialogues

Read the introduction and the gist question for each conversation. Then listen or read the conversation and answer the questions.

1 A GLASS OF TEA, PLEASE

02.05 *Banu and Şafak are cousins. They are sitting at a table in a café in Istanbul by the Bosphorus. A waiter comes to take the order.*

1   What do Banu and Şafak order?

Garson	Buyrun, efendim?
Banu	Bir bardak çay, lütfen.

(The waiter writes down the order and repeats it to check he has written it down correctly.)

Garson	Bir bardak çay. Siz, efendim?

(The waiter turns to Şafak.)

Şafak	Bir bira ve bir şişe su, lütfen.
Garson	Bira yok, efendim.
Şafak	İçecek ne var?

(The waiter hands Şafak a menu.)

Garson	Buyrun, mönü.

(Şafak looks at the menu.)

Şafak	Teşekkür. Bir Nescafé, lütfen.
Garson	Süt?
Şafak	Evet, sütlü.

(The waiter writes down the order and repeats it to check.)

Garson	Bir çay, bir sütlü Nescafé.
Şafak	Evet, tamam.

(The waiter returns with the drinks.)

Garson	Bir çay, bir Nescafé, şeker, süt.
Banu and Şafak	Teşekkürler.
Garson	Afiyet olsun, efendim.

(Şafak calls the waiter and asks for the bill.)

Şafak	Garson!
Garson	Buyrun.
Şafak	Hesap, lütfen.

(They pay the bill and tell the waiter to keep the change.)

Şafak	Üstü kalsın.
Garson	Sağ olun, efendim.

> **TIP**
> It is customary to leave a 10 per cent tip.

2 What drinks are mentioned?

3 How is the instant coffee served?

2 THE COFFEE IS VERY GOOD HERE

 02.06 *A family is sitting at the next table to Banu and Şafak. They are enjoying a day out together. The waiter approaches their table, and they order some drinks.*

1 What do the family members order?

Garson	Buyrun, efendim.
Mother	Bir şekerli kahve.
Father	Bana da şekersiz.

(The mother asks the child what she would like.)

Mother	Sen yavrum? Limonata?

(The child looks at the menu.)

Child	Hayır, ayran, lütfen.
Mother	Tamam.

(The father orders for everyone and the waiter writes it down.)

Father	İki kahve, bir şekerli, bir sade ve bir ayran.
Garson	Tabii, efendim.

(The waiter brings the drinks, which include two glasses of water to go with the coffees.)

Garson	Buyrun efendim, içecekleriniz.
Everyone	Teşekkürler.
Garson	Afiyet olsun.
Mother	Kahveler çok güzel, değil mi?
Father	Evet, çok güzel.
Child	Acıktım.
Mother	Ben de. Tost*?
Child	Evet, peynirli tost ve ayran.

(The father calls the waiter and gives him the order.)

Father	Garson, lütfen.
Garson	Buyrun?
Father	Üç peynirli tost ve üç ayran lütfen.

(While waiting for the food, the mother enjoys the view.)

Mother	Manzara çok güzel, değil mi?
Father	Evet, çok güzel.

***Tost** is a Turkish toasted sandwich.

Ayran is a yogurt drink made by whipping yogurt with water. Especially on hot days it's refreshing, healthy and goes well with meat and pastry dishes or just as a thirst quencher. Every **kebapçı, börekçi** and **büfe** sells **ayran**. People also make **ayran** at home.

2 How are the coffees served?

3 What do they say about the view?

Ordering drinks in Turkish is very easy – all you need to know are your numbers and the names of the drinks. Unlike in English, you don't change the ending on the name of the drink when ordering more than one. So *two teas* is **iki çay**. *Three beers* is **üç bira** and so on. The most difficult part is choosing what you want!

3 ONE RED WINE, PLEASE

 02.07 Banu and Şafak meet in a bar later the same day.

1 What drinks and snacks do Şafak and Banu order?

Şafak	İyi akşamlar.
Garson	İyi akşamlar, efendim. Buyrun?
Banu	Bir şarap, lütfen.
Şafak	Kırmızı mı, beyaz mı?
Banu	Kırmızı, lütfen.
Şafak	Bir kırmızı şarap ve bir rakı lütfen.
Garson	Tabii, efendim. Çerez?
Şafak	Evet, fıstık, biraz da karışık meyve ve beyaz peynir, lütfen.
Garson	Tabii, efendim.

2 Does Banu order red or white wine?

3 What type of cheese do they order?

Language discovery

In Turkish, all nouns (names of things, opinions and feelings, etc.) can be made plural by adding the ending **-ler** or **-lar**. Most Turkish salutations are plural.

akşam *evening*   **akşamlar** *evenings*

1 Underline the *-ler* and *-lar* endings in these salutations.

iyi akşamlar	*good evening*
iyi geceler	*goodnight*
selamlar	*hello*
tebrikler	*congratulations*
mutlu yıllar	*happy new year*
mutlu bayramlar	*have a happy Bayram* (See Unit 9.)
iyi şanslar	*good luck*
iyi yolculuklar	*have a good journey*
iyi günler	*good day*
renkli rüyalar	*sweet dreams*
mutlu Noeller*	*happy Christmas*

***Noel Baba** = *Father Christmas*

2   **You add *-lar* if the last vowel is a, ı, o, u. You add *-ler* if the last vowel is e, i, ö, ü. Now underline the last vowel before *-ler* or *-lar* in the salutations in Question 1.**

3   **Now write the plurals for these nouns from the dialogues.**
   a   kahve
   b   tost
   c   çay
   d   süt

Go further

1 MORE NUMBERS

 02.08 First read and listen to the following numbers; then pause the recording and repeat each number after the speaker. Try saying the numbers from 10 to 20 and then the multiples of 10 to 100 without looking at the book. Next try saying them backwards.

10	**on**	20	**yirmi**
11	**on bir**	30	**otuz**
12	**on iki**	40	**kırk**
13	**on üç**	50	**elli**
14	**on dört**	60	**altmış**
15	**on beş**	70	**yetmiş**
16	**on altı**	80	**seksen**
17	**on yedi**	90	**doksan**
18	**on sekiz**	100	**yüz**
19	**on dokuz**	200	**iki yüz**

To say more numbers, just put the words together: 41 = **kırk bir**.

TIP

In English, we say *one hundred*. In Turkish, we just say **yüz**.

2 RENKLER *COLOURS*

 02.09

beyaz	*white*	**pembe**	*pink*
kırmızı	*red*	**siyah**	*black*
mavi	*blue*	**gri**	*grey*
yeşil	*green*	**mor**	*purple*
sarı	*yellow*	**turuncu**	*orange*

 Can you guess what these combinations mean?

1 kahverengi

2 şaraprengi

3 turkuaz mavi

Hint: ***rengi** means *coloured*; e.g., **kahverengi** is *coffee-coloured*. Look at the vocabulary list at the back of the book.

> **TIP**
>
> **Koyu renk** means *dark in colour* and **açık renk** means *light in colour*. The colour of your tea shows how strong or weak it is:
>
> **koyu çay** or **koyu kahve** = *strong tea* or *strong coffee*
>
> **açık çay** = *weak tea*, but we wouldn't use **açık kahve** unless we mean the colour

3 ASKING QUESTIONS

Did you notice that the mother and the waiter turned the name of a drink into a question, e.g., **Limonata? Çerez?** This would probably sound a bit abrupt in English but is perfectly normal in Turkish. The mother asks her daughter if she would like some lemonade by simply saying **Limonata?** and raising the pitch of her voice at the end of the word. This is a really easy way of making a question in Turkish. Have a go!

4 VAR AND YOK *THERE IS/ARE/NOT*

Var means *there is* or *there are*.

Ne var?	*What's there?/What have you got?*
Çay var.	*There is tea.*
Rakı var.	*There is raki.*

Yok means *there isn't* or *there aren't (any)*.

Ne yok?	*What isn't there?/What haven't you got?*
Kahve yok.	*There isn't any coffee.*
Bira yok.	*There isn't any beer.*

24

Practice

1 What is the Turkish word for these drinks?

2 02.10 **Offer someone a drink by raising the tone of your voice at the end of the word. Listen to the audio to check that you are right.**

Example: **Şarap?**

3 02.11 **Make the following words plural by adding *-ler* or *-lar*. Listen to the audio to check your work.**

Example: **bardak → bardaklar**

a çay

b rakı

c tost

d teşekkür

e bira

f İçecek

4 Put the letters in the correct order to make names of colours.

a sarı

b zabey

c vima

d irkımız

5 What new colour do these colour combinations make?

a mavi + sarı

b kırmızı + sar

c siyah + beyaz

d beyaz + kırmızı

e kırmızı + mavi

6 Look at the following sums. Put a ✓ next to those that are correct (*doğru*) and an ✗ next to those that are wrong (*yanlış*).

a on + yirmi = kırk

b otuz + elli = altmış

c on beş + on beş = otuz

d seksen – kırk = kırk

e yetmiş – elli = on

7 Write the following numbers in figures.

a sıfır

b elli yedi

c on bir

d otuz beş

e yirmi üç

f kırk altı

g altmış

Speaking

 02.12 **Listen to the conversation. Then practise role playing each part.**

In a café

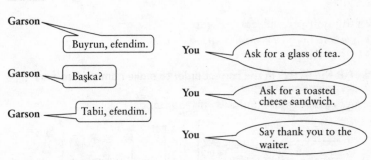

Garson — Buyrun, efendim.

You — Ask for a glass of tea.

Garson — Başka?

You — Ask for a toasted cheese sandwich.

Garson — Tabii, efendim.

You — Say thank you to the waiter.

Test yourself

 02.13 **Listen and answer the following questions orally or in writing.**

1. How do you call the waiter to your table?
2. How do you ask for a Turkish coffee with, or without, sugar?
3. Ask for a white instant coffee.
4. How do you order a glass of tea?
5. Ask for a glass of red wine and a glass of white wine.

SELF CHECK	
	I CAN. . .
⬤	. . . order drinks and snacks.
⬤	. . . ask for a menu or the bill.
⬤	. . . use the numbers 10–100.
⬤	. . . say basic colours.

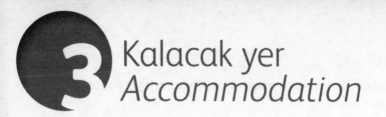

3 Kalacak yer
Accommodation

In this unit you will learn how to:
▶ *enquire about accommodation.*
▶ *ask about facilities.*
▶ *check in and fill in a registration form.*
▶ *say telephone numbers.*
▶ *use numbers for hundreds and thousands.*

CEFR: *(A1) Can use basic phrases and sentences in order to book accommodation, ask about facilities, fill in simple check-in forms.*

Accommodation in Turkey

There are many forms of accommodation that are available when you stay in Turkey. These can include **oteller** (*hotels*), **pansiyonlar** (*guesthouses*) and **kiralık villalar** (*rented villas*) or **apartmanlar** (*apartments*). Whatever you choose depends on what you want from your holiday.

Hotels can be expensive, but you will almost always be provided with facilities such as **internet** (*internet*), meeting rooms and leisure facilities, including swimming pools and **cimnastik salonu** (*gym*). With five-star hotels you can be **garantili lüks** (*guaranteed luxury*) and first-class **servis** (*service*). Make sure you check the **otel web sitesi** (*hotel website*) and online reviews before you book.

Pansiyonlar (*guesthouses*) are a popular choice of accommodation as they are inexpensive. These are ideal for students as they are basic, yet generally well kept. Again it is always best to do your research beforehand.

Staying in rented accommodation such as villas and apartments is a brilliant way to experience Turkish life first hand. These provide both great value for money and the privacy to enjoy your holiday at your own leisure.

1 How would you ask for a hotel?
2 Where would a person with a limited budget choose to stay?

Vocabulary builder

03.01 **Which hotel? Listen and repeat. Then complete the missing parts of the Turkish expressions.**

İşte harita, _____ 'Danışma' ve _____ da 'Yeşil Ev'.

Here is the map, this is the information office and this is 'Yeşil Ev'.

_____ bina galiba.

I think it is that building.

Evet, şubina.

Yes, that is the building.

NEW EXPRESSIONS

Listen to the words and phrases you will hear in the dialogues. Practise listening and saying the expressions until you feel you have learned them.

Dialogue 1 Which hotel?

03.02

kalacak yerler listesi	*lists of accommodation*
otel	*hotel*
pansiyon	*guesthouse*
veya	*or*
kamp	*campsite*
hangi?	*which?*
yakın	*near*
Yeşil Ev	*Green House*

Nasıl yazılır?	*How do you spell it?*
işte	*here*
harita	*map*
bu	*this*
danışma	*information*
ve bu da	*and this is*
harika	*wonderful*
çok	*very*
bina	*building*
acaba	*I wonder*
o	*that* (referring to something relatively far away in this dialogue; **o** with the same spelling also means *he/she/it* as a pronoun)
galiba	*I think*

Dialogue 2 Do you have a vacant room?

 03.03

boş	*vacant*
oda	*room*
kaç kişi?	*how many people?*
kardeşim	*my sister/brother/sibling*
tek kişilik	*a single*
ayrı	*separate*
maalesef	*unfortunately* (a polite remark)
ama	*but*
tek yataklı	*with a single bed*
büyük	*big*
balkonlu	*with a balcony*
deniz	*sea*
manzaralı	*with a view*
banyo	*bathroom*
sıcak	*hot*
su	*water*
hem ... hem	*both ... and*
küvet	*bath tub*
duş	*shower*
her zaman	*always*

ne kadar?	how much?
kahvaltı	breakfast
dahil/dahil mi?	included/is it included?
tamam	OK
kaç?	how many?
pasaport	passport
işte	here it is
doğum yeri	place of birth
doğum tarihi	date of birth
milliyet	nationality
pasaport numarası	passport number
numara	number
anahtar	key
valiz	suitcase

Dialogue 3 There are lots of good campsites

03.04

biraz	a little
pahalı	expensive
ucuz	cheap
liste	list
adres	address
telefon numaraları	telephone numbers
orada	there
kart	card
alo	hello (on the phone)
çadır	tent
kaç günlük?	how many days?
kampta	at the campsite
elektrik	electricity
devamlı	continuous
yüzme-havuzu	swimming pool
ilk yardım	first-aid post
plaj	beach
çocuk	child
oyun parkı	play area
genel telefon	public phone
da	also

yarın	tomorrow
sabah	morning
görüşürüz	see you
adınız	your name
adım	my name (first name)
soyadım	my surname
efendim?	pardon?
tekrar	again

Dialogue 4 This is your tent

03.05

hoş geldiniz	welcome
hoş bulduk	set reply to **hoş geldiniz**
iyiyiz	we are well
meşgulüz	we are busy
sizin	your
burası	here, this place
şurası	there, that place
bunlar	these are
şunlar	those are
bungalov	bungalow
köpek	dog

Question words and phrases

03.06

hangi?	which?
ne?	what?
ne kadar?	how much?
var mı?	is there?/have you got?
nasıl?	how?/what is it like?
nasılsınız?	how are you?
kaç kişi?	how many people?
kim?	who?
kaç günlük?	how many days?
kaça?	how much?

Dialogues

Read the introduction and the gist question for each conversation. Then listen or read the conversation and answer the questions.

1 WHICH HOTEL?

03.07 *Ben and Laura, a brother and sister in their early thirties, are visiting Istanbul. They are at the tourist office in Sultan Ahmet Square looking for accommodation.*

1 What does Ben want?

Ben	Merhaba.
Memur*	Merhaba efendim.
Ben	Kalacak yerler listesi var mı, lütfen?
Memur	Otel, pansiyon veya kamp?
Ben	Otel, lütfen.
Memur	Buyrun.
Ben	Hangi otel yakın?
Memur	'Yeşil Ev' çok yakın.
Ben	Nasıl yazılır, lütfen?
Memur	Y – e – ş – i – l – E – v.
Ben	Teşekkürler.
Memur	İşte harita, bu 'Danışma' ve bu da 'Yeşil Ev'.
Ben	Ah! Harika, çok teşekkürler.
(They walk towards the hotel. Ben wonders which building the hotel is.)	
Ben	Hangi bina acaba?
Laura	Şu bina galiba.
(Ben reads the sign above the hotel.)	
Ben	Evet, o bina.

***memur** = *civil servant*

2 Which accommodation is nearby?

3 What type of accommodation is Yeşil Ev?

2 DO YOU HAVE A VACANT ROOM?

 03.08 *Ben and Laura enter the hotel and are at the reception desk.*

> **TIP**
>
> Note that **resepsiyon** is commonly used in big international hotels; it is borrowed
> from French. **Resepsiyon memuru** means *receptionist* and **resepsiyon masası**
> means *reception desk*.

1 What are they making enquiries about?

Ben	İyi akşamlar.
Receptionist	İyi akşamlar, efendim.
Ben	Boş oda var mı?
Receptionist	Kaç kişi?
Ben	Ben ve kardeşim, tek kişilik, iki ayrı oda.
Receptionist	Maalesef, tek kişilik iki oda yok. Ama iki tek yataklı büyük bir oda var.

(Ben and Laura are undecided, so the receptionist shows them the room.)

Receptionist	Balkonlu ve deniz manzaralı.
Laura	Banyo ve sıcak su var mı?
Receptionist	Evet. Hem küvet hem duş var. Her zaman sıcak su var.
Ben	*(to Laura)* Bu oda güzel, değil mi?
Laura	Evet. Ne kadar?
Receptionist	120 dolar.
Laura	Kahvaltı dahil mi?
Receptionist	Evet, kahvaltı dahil.
Laura	Evet. Tamam.

(They go back down to reception.)

Receptionist	Kaç gece?
Ben	Üç gece.
Receptionist	Pasaportlar, lütfen?
Ben	Tabii, işte pasaportlar.

(They put the passports on the counter.)

Receptionist	Teşekkürler.

(The receptionist starts filling in the hotel forms. While doing so she repeats some of the sections of the form out loud.)

Receptionist	Doğum yeri ... doğum tarihi ... milliyet ... pasaport numarası ... *(turning to Ben and Laura)* Oda, 24 numara.

(She hands them the key for room number 24.)

Receptionist	Buyrun, anahtar.
Laura	Valizler?
Receptionist	Mehmet! *(She calls Mehmet, the porter, to carry their suitcases.)*

2 For how many nights do they want the room?

3 Is breakfast included in the price?

3 WHAT FACILITIES DO YOU HAVE?

03.09 *Banu and Şafak are at a tourist information office in Izmir enquiring about accommodation.*

1 **What type of place does Banu call?**

Şafak	Merhaba.
Clerk	İyi günler.
Şafak	Kalacak otel ve kamp listesi var mı?
Clerk	Var. Bu otel listesi.
(They both look at the list.)	
Banu	Oteller biraz pahalı.
Clerk	Çok güzel kamplar var ve çok ucuz. Buyrun işte bu liste. Adresler ve telefon numaraları.
(Banu asks politely if there is a telephone at the office.)	
Banu	Telefon var mı acaba?
Clerk	Evet. İşte orada. *(The clerk points out the telephone.)*
Şafak	Kart var mı?*
Clerk	Evet. 50 kontür 3,75 lira, 350 kontör 19,00 TL.
Şafak	Bir kart, lütfen.
(The clerk gives him the telephone card. He dials the number.)	
Kamp	Alo ... 752 52 06 Truva Kamping. Buyrun.
Şafak	Alo. Ben Şafak Gezer. İki kişilik çadır var mı?
Kamp	Evet, var. Kaç günlük?
Şafak	Beş gün.
Kamp	Tamam.
Şafak	Kampta neler var? Elektrik var mı?
Kamp	Tabii. Devamlı elektrik, su ve sıcak su var. Restoran, yüzme-havuzu, plaj, duşlar, çocuk oyun parkı, ilk yardım ve genel telefon da var.
Şafak	Tamam. Yarın sabah görüşürüz.
Kamp	Tamam. Adınız, lütfen?
Şafak	Adım Şafak, soyadım Gezer.
Kamp	Efendim? Nasıl yazılır?
Şafak	Ş – a – f – a – k – G – e – z – e – r.

*You need a telephone card to use a public telephone in Turkey.

2 How does Banu ask to use the phone?

3 Can they rent a tent too?

4 THIS IS YOUR TENT

 03.10 Next day Banu and Şafak arrive at the campsite and the manager Ayşegül meets them.

1 What expression tells you the campsite is busy?

Ayşegül	Ben Ayşegül. Hoş geldiniz.
Banu	Ben Banu. *(Points at Şafak.)* O Şafak. *(They shake hands.)*
Banu and Şafak	Hoş bulduk.
Ayşegül	Nasılsınız?
Banu	Biz iyiyiz, teşekkürler. Siz nasılsınız?

(Ayşegül smiles.)

Ayşegül	Çok meşgulüz.

(Ayşegül shows them their tent and the facilities of the campsite.)

Ayşegül	Bu sizin çadır, burası araba parkı, o telefon, şurası yüzme-havuzu ve şu restoran, bunlar tuvaletler, şunlar duşlar, bu bungalov ilk yardım.

(They hear a dog barking.)

Ayşegül	O da bizim köpek Karabaş.

(They all laugh.)

*Karabaş is a very common name for a dog in Turkish and literally means black head.

hav-hav

2   **What facilities are at the campsite?**

3   **What does Ayşegül say about free time?**

Language discovery

1   **Answer these questions about the dialogues. Use Turkish where possible.**

   a   How does Ben say *how do you spell it, please?*
   b   How does Ben ask *is there a vacant room?*
   c   How does Şafak ask *is there a tent for two people?*
   d   How does Ayşegül say *we're very busy?*

2   **Find the campsite phone number in the dialogue. How does the speaker break down the number?**

3   **What does this sign mean?**

Dikkat
köpek
var!

Go further

1 SPELLING WORDS

When booking accommodation or tickets, you may be asked to spell your name, or you may want to know how the name of a hotel or other location is spelled. The question to ask about the spelling of a word is simply **Nasıl yazılır?**

Review the letters of the **Türkçe alfabe** (*Turkish alphabet*) in **The alphabet and pronunciation** section. Practise the question, and practise spelling your name and various place names and addresses.

2 KAÇ? *HOW MANY? HOW MUCH?*

Kaç is a useful little word which means *how many?* or *how much?*

Kaç lira?	*How many lira?*
Kaç gece?	*How many nights?*
Kaç kişi?	*How many people?*
Kaç gün?	*How many days?*

3 MORE NUMBERS – HUNDREDS AND THOUSANDS

 03.11 First read and listen to these numbers, then pause the audio and repeat each number after the speaker. Try saying the numbers from 100 to 9,000, then try saying them from 9,000 down to 100.

100	yüz	1,000	bin
200	ikiyüz	2,000	ikibin
300	üçyüz	3,000	üçbin
400	dörtyüz	4,000	dörtbin
500	beşyüz	5,000	beşbin
600	altıyüz	6,000	altıbin
700	yediyüz	7,000	yedibin
800	sekizyüz	8,000	sekizbin
900	dokuzyüz	9,000	dokuzbin

4 TELEPHONE NUMBERS

Turkish telephone numbers usually have seven digits, plus an area code where appropriate. When giving a telephone number, it is usual to break it down into three digits, two digits and two digits. Practise saying these phone numbers.

Dedeman Hotel 337 45 00　　　　　Yeşil Ev Hotel 517 67 85

> **TIP**
>
> If you're calling the Dedeman Hotel in Istanbul from England, you need to dial: 00 90 0212 337 45 00.
> 00 international code - 90 for Turkey - 0212 for Istanbul - 337 45 00 Dedeman Hotel
> If you're calling the Yeşil Ev Hotel in Istanbul and you're in Istanbul, you don't need to dial **Istanbul kod** *the code for Istanbul*: (0212) 517 517 67 85.

5 PERSONAL PRONOUNS

A pronoun is a word that is used instead of a noun. Here is the table of subject pronouns.

ben	*I*	**biz**	*we*
sen	*you* (singular)	**siz**	*you* (plural)
o	*he, she, it*	**onlar**	*they*

You learned about **sen** and **siz** in Unit 1, and now you have encountered some of the other personal pronouns (**ben**, **biz**, **o**). In the dialogue, Banu introduces herself by saying **Ben Banu** (*I am Banu*); Banu and Şafak say **Biz iyiyiz** (*We are fine*) and Ayşegül introduces the dog by saying **O da bizim köpek Karabaş**. You probably noticed one way that Turkish is simpler than English – no words for *am*, *are* or *is* are needed! In other words, there is no verb *to be*.

6 BU, ŞU, O *THIS, THAT*

Where English has two words for *this* and *that*, Turkish has three: **bu, şu, o**. **Bu** means *this* as in **Bu sizin çadır** (*This is your tent*), when it is very near. **Şu** means *that* when you are referring to something fairly near. **O** means *that* when you are referring to something further away. So when Ayşegül says **Şu bungalov, o telefon** she is indicating that the bungalow is a little way off and the telephone is further away.

Again, no words are used for *is* or *are*; e.g., **Bu çadır** (*This is the tent*). However, you do need to add the plural ending on **bu, şu** or **o** if you are referring to plural nouns. As an example, Ayşegül says **bunlar tuvaletler** (*these are the toilets*).

 Look at the words in the table below. Describe how we make them plural.

Singular	Plural
bu	bunlar
şu	şunlar
o	onlar

7 WORD ORDER

Turkish word order is, generally speaking, flexible, but note that moving the **o** can change the meaning of your sentence. For example:

O kim?	*Who is that person?*
Kim o?	*Who is there?*

8 BURASI, ŞURASI, ORASI *THIS/THAT PLACE*

Listen to the audio and read the dialogue again. You heard Ayşegül say, **Burası araba parkı** *This (place) is the car park.*

Three useful words are **burası, şurası** and **orası**.

 Can you figure out what words they are derived from? Can you guess what these new words mean?

9 TONGUE TWISTER

 03.12 Try this Turkish tongue twister:

Şu şişe su şişesi, şu şişe süt şişesi. *This bottle is (a) water bottle, this bottle is (a) milk bottle.*

10 BORROWED WORDS

Here are some words used in this unit borrowed mostly from English and French. Look back at the dialogues and find the words. Can you work out the meanings in the dialogues?

> otel pansiyon resepsiyon liste kamp
> telefon duş pasaport balkon adres elektrik
> restoran kart plaj park tuvalet bungalov

Practice

1 03.13 **Read these telephone numbers for Turkish campsites out loud. Then compare with the audio. For more practice, write down the numbers in words.**

Example: **Incekum 345 14 48 üçyüzkırkbeş ondört kırksekiz**

   a Gökova 246 50 35

   b Çamlıköy 262 01 37

   c Yat 614 13 33

   d V – Camp 717 22 24

   e Pamukcak 896 36 36

   f Altınkum Camp 311 48 57

2 **Write these numbers in figures.**

   a beşyüzotuzbir

   b dörtyüzkırkdört

   c altıbinyediyüzellibeş

   d binbir

   e üçbinotuzüç

   f dokuzyüzonaltı

   g yedibinsekizyüzondört

   h dörtbin

3 **Match the words on the left with the pictures on the right. The first one has been done for you.**

a gölgelik

b elektrik

c restoran

d su

e yüzme-havuzu

f ilk yardım

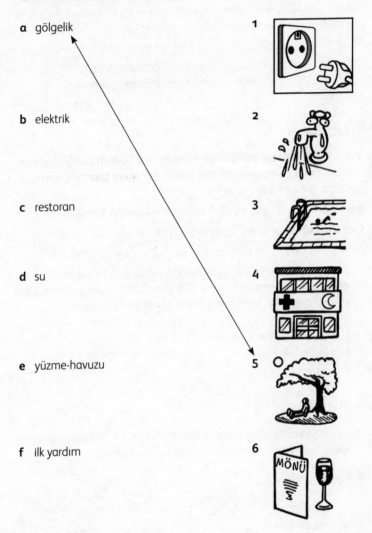

4 Complete the hotel registration form with your own (or invented) information.

Ad:	....
Soyadı:	....
Yaş:	....
E-Posta:	....
GSM:	....
Adres:	....
Pasaport numarası:	....

ad = *name*　　**soyad** = *surname*
yaş = *age*

 Can you work out what these words mean?

a GSM　　　　b Adres　　　c Pasaport numarası

5 Reorder the following sentences to make a dialogue. We have given you the first sentence. The punctuation will give you clues. (The dialogue is between a hotel guest and the doorman.)

a ___ Buyrun?　　　　　　　　e _1_ Afedersiniz.
b ___ Araba parkı var mı acaba?　f ___ Şurada.
c ___ Nerede?　　　　　　　　g ___ Teşekkürler.
d ___ Var efendim.

Speaking

 1 03.14 Listen to the conversation between a hotel guest and the receptionist. Then practise role playing each part.

Resepsiyon memuru — Hoş geldiniz. | Siz — Reply to the receptionist's welcome and ask if they have a vacant room.

Resepsiyon memuru — Evet, var. | Siz — Say you want a single room.

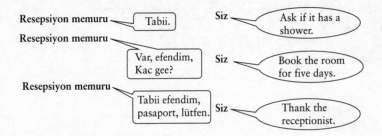

Resepsiyon memuru	Tabii.	Siz	Ask if it has a shower.
Resepsiyon memuru	Var, efendim, Kac gee?	Siz	Book the room for five days.
Resepsiyon memuru	Tabii efendim, pasaport, lütfen.	Siz	Thank the receptionist.

? Test yourself

03.15 Listen and answer the following questions orally or in writing.

a Ask for a room with a shower.

b Ask whether the hotel has a vacant room.

c Ask if breakfast is included.

d Ask someone how you spell a word.

e How do you say this and that?

If you get any wrong, go back through the unit and have another look before moving on to the next unit.

SELF CHECK

I CAN...
... enquire about accommodation.
... ask about facilities.
... check in and fill in a registration form.
... say telephone numbers.
... use numbers for hundreds and thousands.

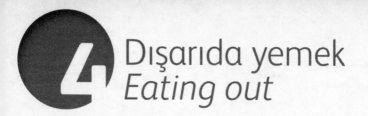

Dışarıda yemek
Eating out

In this unit you will learn how to:
▶ *order meals.*
▶ *enquire about dishes and what's in them.*
▶ *pay the bill and leave a tip.*

CEFR: *(A1) Can communicate in simple sentences to order meals, enquire what's in dishes, pay the bill and leave a tip.*

 Turkish cuisine

The Turks are very creative when it comes to food. **Sebze** (*vegetables*), **et** (*meat*), **pilav** (*cooked rice, vermicelli or cracked wheat, plain or with small pieces of vegetables or meat*) and **börek** (*pastry*) are the main features of Turkish cuisine. **Ekmek** (*bread*) is served with almost everything, as is a glass of **su** (*water*).

Börek are delicious savouries made of thin layers of dough with meat, vegetable, cheese or onion fillings. They are baked or fried. You can find them at a **börekçi** (*pastry shop*), **pastane** (*cake shop*) or **fırın** (*bakery*).

Other foods to look for include **pide** (*Turkish pizza*), made of flat bread with various toppings, and **lahmacun** (*savoury pancakes*). Both are served in a **pideci** (*Turkish pizza restaurant*). Vegetable dishes are plentiful, but strict vegetarians should ask for them to be **zeytinyağlı** (*cooked with olive oil*) rather than meat stock. If you want to ask what vegetarian options are available, ask **Etsiz yemek ne var?** (*What vegetarian dishes do you have?*)

In Turkish, two words are used for restaurant – **restoran** and **lokanta**. **Restoran** is more common in tourist areas and big cities, and the restaurants are usually proud to display their star ratings at the entrance and on the menu: **lüks** (*luxury*), **1'inci sınıf** (*first class*), **2'nci sınıf** (*second class*). **Lokanta** is more often used for local or rural restaurants and cafés. Restaurant prices include **KDV** (*VAT*). A 10 per cent **bahşiş** (*tip*) is customary and much appreciated.

1 **What do Turkish people have with almost every meal?**
2 **If you are vegetarian, how would you enquire about food?**

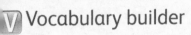 Vocabulary builder

YER/MEVKİ *LOCATIONS*

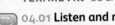 04.01 **Listen and repeat. Then complete the missing parts of the Turkish expressions for locations.**

nerede?	*where?*
bahçe _____	*in the garden*
kahvaltı _____	*at breakfast*
masa _____	*at the table*
burada _____ *	*here (in here)*
sağ _____	*on the right*

*In spoken Turkish, generally **burada** becomes **burda**.

NEW EXPRESSIONS

Listen to the words and phrases you will hear in the dialogues. Practise listening and saying the names of the food and drinks and the expressions until you feel you have learned them.

Dialogue 1 Ordering breakfast

 04.02

hava	*weather*
bizim için	*for us*
Türk kahvaltısı	*Turkish breakfast*
neler?	*what is there?*
tereyağı	*butter*
bal	*honey*
marmelat	*marmalade*
reçel	*jam*
peynir	*cheese*
zeytin	*olives*
sosis	*sausage*
sucuk	*spicy Turkish sausage*
salam	*salami*
domates	*tomatoes*
salatalık	*cucumber*
biber	*pepper*
taze	*fresh*
ekmek	*bread*

yumurta	*egg*
bana	*for me*
rafadan	*soft-boiled egg*
da	*also, two (separate)*
lezzetli	*tasty*
tuz	*salt*
kızarmış	*toasted*
Başka?	*Anything else?*
yok	*no, not, there isn't*

Dialogue 2 At a fish restaurant

04.03

Ya sen?	*And you?*
vişne suyu	*sour cherry juice*
hemen	*straightaway*
balık	*fish*
karışık salata	*mixed salad*
dilimlenmiş	*sliced*
kalkan tava	*fried turbot*
karışık salata	*mixed salad*
levrek buğulama	*steamed bass*
barbunya tava	*fried red mullet*
lüfer ızgara	*grilled blue fish*
dilimlenmiş	*sliced*
roka	*rocket leaves*
Üstü kalsın.	*Keep the change.*
taksi	*taxi*

Dialogue 3 At a köfte restaurant

04.04

öğlen	*noon*
hadi	*come on*
cız bız	*sizzling/fried*
porsiyon	*portion*
pilavlı	*with cooked rice*
benim için	*for me*
bana da	*for me too*
başka	*anything else*
piyaz	*white bean salad*

Dialogues

**Read the introduction and the gist question for each conversation.
Then listen or read the conversation and answer the questions.**

1 ORDERING BREAKFAST

04.05 *Ben and Laura decide to have
a typical Turkish breakfast in the
hotel garden.*

> **TIP**
>
> A typical Turkish **kahvaltı** (*breakfast*) consists of **çay** (*tea*), with **ekmek** (*bread*) or
> **kızarmış ekmek** (*toast*, literally *reddened bread*), **tereyağı** (*butter*), **bal** (*honey*) or
> **reçel** (*jam*). **Gül reçeli** (*rose petal jam*), **incir reçeli** (*fig jam*) and **vişne reçeli** (*sour
> cherry jam*) are worth trying. **Peynir** (*cheese*) and **zeytin** (*olives*) are usually served
> at breakfast, too. You can also ask for **yumurta** (*eggs*), either **rafadan** (*soft boiled*),
> **katı** (*hard boiled*) or **yağda** (*fried*).

1 What kind of breakfast would they like to have?

Laura	Bahçede kahvaltı çok hoş.
Ben	Evet. Hava ne güzel!
Garson	Günaydın, efendim.
Ben	Günaydın. Bizim için Türk kahvaltısı, lütfen.
Garson	Tabii, efendim.
Laura	Kahvaltıda neler var?

(The waiter brings the breakfast on a trolley.)

Garson	Tereyağı, bal, marmelat, reçel, peynir, zeytin, sosis.
Ben	Sucuk yok mu?
Garson	Var, efendim. Salam, domates, salatalık, biber. Ve taze ekmek de var tabii.
Ben	Çay var mı?
Garson	Tabii.

(He pours their tea into tulip-shaped glasses.)

Laura	Teşekkürler.

(Laura has a sip of the tea.)

Laura	Çay çok lezzetli.
Garson	Afiyet olsun, efendim.

(The waiter puts the breakfast on the table.)

Garson	Yumurta?
Laura	Hayır, teşekkürler.
Ben	Evet, bana rafadan lütfen.
Garson	Tabii, efendim.
Ben	Sucuk da çok lezzetli.
Laura	Tuz yok mu?
Ben	İşte masada canım.

(The waiter puts the toast on the table.)

Garson	Buyrun, kızarmış ekmekler de burada. Afiyet olsun. Başka?
Laura	Yok. Teşekkürler.

2 What is the weather like?

3 How does Ben want his egg?

2 AT A FISH RESTAURANT

 04.06 *Ahmet and Yeşim decide to go to a **balık restoranı** (fish restaurant) with their friends Vanessa and Asuman. Yeşim makes the reservation for four people and they meet at the restaurant at 8 p.m. As they are going to have a few drinks, Ahmet does not take his car.*

1 How do you know they are at a fish restaurant?

Ahmet	Garson, lütfen.
Garson	Buyrun, efendim.
Ahmet	Şarap ne var?
Garson	Çankaya ve Kutman çok güzel.
Yeşim	Çankaya, lütfen.
Asuman	Bana da beyaz Çankaya, lütfen.
Ahmet	Ya sen, Vanessa?
Vanessa	Vişne suyu, lütfen.

(Ahmet orders the drinks first.)

Ahmet	Bir büyük beyaz Çankaya. Bir küçük rakı ve bir de vişne suyu.
Garson	Hemen, efendim.
Ahmet	Bir şişe de su tabii.

*(The waiter goes to fetch the drinks. They look at the **balık mönü** (fish menu) and are ready to order when the waiter returns.)*

Ahmet	Bana kalkan tava ve karışık salata, lütfen.
Asuman	Bana levrek buğulama ve yeşil salata, lütfen.
Vanessa	Bana da barbunya tava ve dilimlenmiş domates, lütfen.
Yeşim	Lüfer ızgara ve roka, lütfen.
Garson	Tabii, efendim.

*(They all enjoy their meal. At the end of the meal they have **karışık meyve** (mixed fruit) followed by **Türk kahvesi** (Turkish coffee).)*

Ahmet	Garson, hesap, lütfen.
Garson	Buyrun, hesap.

(Ahmet pays the bill and leaves a tip.)

Ahmet	Teşekkürler. Üstü kalsın.

(The waiter is pleased with the tip.)

Garson	Sağ olun, efendim.
Ahmet	Taksi nerede?
Garson	Burada, sağda, efendim.

2 **What drink does Vanessa order?**

3 **Who orders a green salad?**

3 AT A KÖFTE RESTAURANT

04.07 *Following their visit to the Basilica cistern (a Byzantine underground reservoir) Ben and Laura are now feeling hungry. They can't decide whether to have lunch at a **köfte** restaurant, which specialises in various types of meatballs, or **muhallebici** (shops which sell puddings and savoury pastries).*

1 What type of food do they decide to get?

Ben	Muhallebici mi, köfteci mi?
Laura	Öğlen köfteci, akşam muhallebici.
Ben	Tamam. Hadi.

*(They go to the famous Sultan Ahmet Köftecisi, which overlooks the Blue Mosque. They ask if the restaurant has **cız bız köfte** (grilled meatballs).)*

Ben	Cız bız köfte var mı?
Garson	Var, efendim. Kaç porsiyon?
Laura	İki porsiyon, pilavlı.
Garson	Tabii, efendim.
Laura	*(to Ben)* Bira mı, ayran mı?
Ben	Bira soğuk mu?
Garson	Evet, çok soğuk.
Ben	Benim için, bir soğuk bira.
Laura	Bana da bir soğuk ayran, lütfen.
Garson	Başka?

(They look at the menu.)

Ben	Piyaz var mı?
Garson	Var, efendim.
Ben	Bana bir piyaz.
Laura	Bana da karışık salata.

(The waiter brings their order to the table.)

Garson	Afiyet olsun.
Ben and Laura	Teşekkür! Teşekkürler!
Laura	Köfte çok lezzetli, değil mi?
Ben	Evet, çok.

2 What does Ben want to drink?

3 What kind of salad does Laura want to eat?

💡 Language discovery

1 Answer these questions about the dialogues. Use Turkish where possible.

   a How does Ben say *Turkish breakfast for us, please*?

   b How does Laura enquire what they have for breakfast?

   c How does Ahmet ask for the bill?

   d How does the waiter say where the taxi is?

   e How does Ben ask if the beer is cold?

2 **Find the following two sentences in Dialogue 1. Which ending is on the first word in each, -de or -da?**
  a Bahçe _____ kahvaltı çok hoş.
  b Kahvaltı _____ neler var?
  c What determines the ending?

Go further

1 THE ENDINGS -DE AND -DA FOR LOCATIONS

In Turkish, to say *at, on* or *in* you put the ending **-de**, **-da** on the noun instead of using a separate word. You can translate the two endings as *at, on* or *in*, depending on the context. Look at these examples with **-de** and **-da**.

nerede?	*where?*
bahçede	*in the garden (lit. garden in)*
kahvaltıda	*at breakfast (lit. breakfast at)*
masada	*at the table (lit. table at)*
burada	*here, in here*
sağda	*on the right*
Kahvaltı masada.	*Breakfast is on the table. (lit. Breakfast table on.)*
Kahvaltıda neler var?	*What is there for breakfast? (lit. Is there for breakfast what?)*
restoranda	*at the restaurant (lit. restaurant at)*
otelde	*at the hotel (lit. hotel at)*

2 VOWEL HARMONY

To decide whether to use **-de** or **-da** on the end of a word, you simply choose the one which harmonises best with the last vowel in that word.
▶ **da** harmonises best with (**a, ı, o, u**)
▶ **de** harmonises best with (**e, i, ö, ü**).

It helps if you can remember these vowel groups, but don't worry too much about it. The more you are exposed to the language (particularly the more you hear it and see it), the easier it will become to know which ending to use.

This is the same principle of vowel harmony as with the **-ler, -lar** endings in Unit 2.

3 QUESTIONS WITH *MI, MI, MU* OR *MÜ*

Notice the following questions. What words – **mı, mi, mu** or **mü** – come at the end of each question? The first one is done for you. Notice how they are being used.

1 Üzüm ___mü___?   *(Is it) grapes?*

2 Çay var _____?   *(Is there) tea?*

3 Soğuk _____?   *(Is it) cold?*

4 Köfte çok lezzetli, değil _____?   *Köfte is very tasty, isn't it?*

In general, **mı, mi, mu, mü** appear at the end to make a question. The question words can follow nouns, verbs or adjectives. The following examples use the word with same vowel as the last vowel in the previous word:

Balık mı?   *(Is it) fish?*

Şeftali mi?   *(Is it) a peach?*

Karpuz mu?   *(Is it) watermelon?*

Üzüm mü?   *(Are they) grapes?*

If the last vowel of the preceding word is **a**, **e**, **o** or **ö**, you use the form which sounds the closest. For example:

Çay mı?   *Tea?*

Ekmek mi?   *Bread?*

Tost mu?   *Toasted sandwich?*

Likör mü?   *Liqueur?*

- ▶ **mı** comes after **ı, a**
- ▶ **mi** comes after **i, e**
- ▶ **mu** comes after **u, o**
- ▶ **mü** comes after **ü, ö**

This is another instance of vowel harmony.

Practice

1 Memory game. Study the picture of the breakfast table for three minutes. Then without looking at the page, write down in Turkish what was on the table.

When you can't remember any more items, have another look at the picture for a further two minutes and then write down anything you missed.

2 Complete the questions using *-mı, -mi, -mu* or *-mü*. You may need to use each word more than once.

a Kahvaltı güzel _____?

b Karışık meyve _____?

c Balık lezetli _____?

d Pide ucuz _____?

e O biber mi, tuz _____?

f Otel lüks _____?

3 Reorder the sentences below to form a conversation. Start with Garson.

a __1__ Garson.

b ___ Karışık meyve var mı?

c ___ Bir karışık meyve, lütfen.

d ___ Buyrun?

e ___ Var.

f ___ Tabii efendim.

4 Look at the picture and complete the accompanying sentences.

a Bir bardak _____, lütfen.
b İki porsiyon _____, lütfen.
c Karışık _____, lütfen.
d Daha _____, lütfen.

5 Answer these questions with *evet* (*yes*) or *hayır* (*no*) sentences. Use the emoticon to guide you. The first one has been done for you.

a Yeşil Ev İstanbul'da mı?   ☺   <u>Evet, İstanbul'da.</u>
b Rakı soğuk mu?   ☺   _____
c Döner et mi?   ☺   _____
d Karpuz ucuz mu?   ☺   _____
e Şeftali sebze mi?   ☹   _____
f Salata lezzetli mi?   ☹   _____
g Lokum alkollü mü?   ☹   _____
h Baklava tatlı mı?   ☺   _____
i Zeytin siyah mı?   ☺   _____
j Simit taze mi?   ☺   _____

6 Match the Turkish words with the corresponding picture. The first one has been done for you.

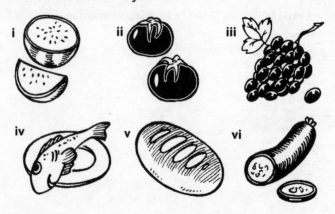

i   ii   iii

iv   v   vi

7 **Complete each conversation. Use the endings and words in the box.**

-de	-da	mı	mi	mu	mü

a A: Açık hava _____ kahvaltı ne güzel.
   B: Evet. Hava ne güzel.
b A: Taksi var _____?
   B: Bura, _____, efendim.
c A: Tuz yok _____?
   B: İşte masa _____ canım.
d A: Köfte var _____?
   B: Var efendim. Kaç porsiyon?
e A: Bira soğuk _____?
   B: Evet, çok soğuk.

 Speaking

04.08 **You are in a Turkish pizza restaurant. Listen to the conversation. Then practise role playing each part.**

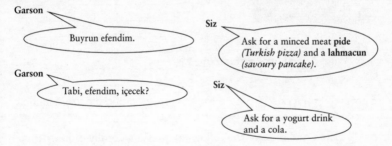

Garson

Buyrun efendim.

Siz

Ask for a minced meat **pide** (*Turkish pizza*) and a **lahmacun** (*savoury pancake*).

Garson

Tabi, efendim, içecek?

Siz

Ask for a yogurt drink and a cola.

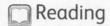 Reading

Look at the text message and answer the questions. Try to use Turkish.

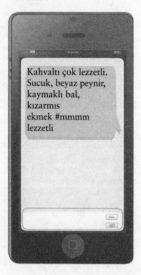

Kahvaltı çok lezzetli.
Sucuk, beyaz peynir,
kaymaklı bal,
kızarmış
ekmek #mmmm
lezzetli

1 What is breakfast like?
2 What do you think **mmmm** means?

 Test yourself

 04.09 **Listen and answer the following questions orally or in writing.**

1 Order a breakfast of coffee, butter, bread, sausages and egg.
2 Order fried fish with a green salad.
3 Order a large white wine.
4 Order two portions of meatballs with cooked rice.
5 Ask if the beer is cold.

If you get any wrong, go back through the unit and have another look before moving on to the next unit.

SELF CHECK

I CAN...

...order meals.
...enquire about dishes and what's in them.
...pay the bill and leave a tip.

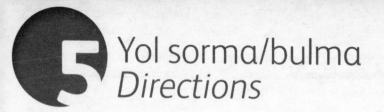

5 Yol sorma/bulma
Directions

In this unit you will learn how to:
▸ *ask for and give directions.*
▸ *get around a new place.*
▸ *ask what something means.*
▸ *ask when something is open.*

CEFR: *(A2) Can communicate in a simple and direct exchange of information on familiar matters such as: ask for and give directions, understand warning signs, get around a new place and ask what something means. Enquire about when somewhere is open. Can use verbs in instruction forms.*

Asking for directions

General information about Turkey and basic **haritalar** (*maps*) are available from the Turkish **turizm bürosu** (*tourist offices*), abroad and in Turkey. When you need to ask something, the easiest way to attract someone's attention is to say **Afedersiniz** (*excuse me*) followed by your question. To ask where something is, say the word for what you are looking for, followed by **nerede** (*where*); e.g., **Giriş nerede?** (*Where is the entrance?*), **Gişe nerede?** (*Where is the ticket office?*). When you're being given directions, listen for the important bits such as whether to **sağa dön** (*turn right*) or **sola dön** (*turn left*), and try to repeat each bit to make sure you have understood it correctly. You can always ask the person to say it again more slowly: **bir daha lütfen** (*once more please*); **daha yavaş** (*more slowly*). If you are looking for a **tuvalet** (*toilet*), they are sometimes labelled **baylar** (*gentlemen*) and **bayanlar** (*ladies*) or **erkek** (*men*) and **kadın** (*women*). They may also be marked with the sign **00**.

1 **How would you ask where the toilets are?**
2 **You see a sign with oo on it. What is that?**

Vocabulary builder

COGNATES

 05.01 **These are all English cognates, words that have similar sounds and meanings in Turkish and English. Listen to these words in Turkish and repeat them. Then write down what you think the English words are.**

banka	_____
pasaport	_____
kontrol	_____
taksi	_____
kilometre	_____
harem	_____
kart	_____

VERBS

 05.02 **Listen to and read some verbs you will hear in the dialogues. These are all polite commands. Practise saying them until you feel you have learned them.**

sorun	*ask* (polite)
gidin	*go* (polite)
dönün	*turn/return* (polite)
çıkın	*go out* (polite)
geçin	*cross* (polite)
bırakın	*leave* (polite)

NEW EXPRESSIONS

Listen to the words and phrases you will hear in the dialogues. Practise listening and saying the expressions until you feel you have learned them.

Dialogue 1 At the airport

 05.03

bilmiyorum	*I don't know* (lit. *I am not knowing*)
düz	*straight*
gümrük	*customs*
-den/-dan sonra	*after*
-den/-dan önce	*before*
sağ	*right*
sol	*left*
en	*most*
en yakın	*nearest*
daha	*more*
kapı	*door*
yol	*road*
uzak	*far*
biraz	*a little*
dakika	*minute*
falan	*roughly/or so*

Dialogue 2 In Sultan Ahmet Square

 05.04

Topkapı Müzesi*	*Topkapı Museum*
köşe	*corner*
tam	*right/exactly*
karşı	*opposite*
zaman	*time*
açık	*open*
-den ... -e kadar	*from ... to*
bilet	*ticket*
çanta	*bag*
buraya	*here* (shows movement)
işaret	*sign*

*****Topkapı Müzesi** is also known as **Topkapı Sarayı** meaning *Topkapi Palace*.

Dialogue 3 The Blue Cruise

05.05

Mavi Yolculuk	*Blue Cruise*
nereye?	*where? where to?* (indicates movement)
birinci*	*first*
ikinci*	*second*
liman	*port*
sahil	*coast*
merkez	*centre*
rica ederim	*not at all*

*In the spoken language, **birinci/birincisi** and **ikinci/ikincisi** are used interchangeably.

Dialogues

Read the introduction and the gist question for each conversation. Then listen or read the conversation and answer the questions.

1 AT THE AIRPORT

 05.06 *Dr Bahadır Bey and his wife Ülkü have just landed at **İstanbul Havalimanı** (Istanbul Airport).*

1 What three things are they looking for?

Bahadır	Afedersiniz, banka nerede, acaba?
Passer-by	Özür dilerim. Bilmiyorum. Danışmaya sorun. Danışma orada.
Bahadır	Çok teşekkürler.

(They stop at the information desk.)

Ülkü	Afedersiniz, banka nerede acaba?
Clerk	Düz gidin, pasaport kontrolü geçin ve gümrüklerden sonra sağa dönün, tekrar düz gidin, solda.
Ülkü	Aaa, çok teşekkürler. En yakın tuvalet nerede, acaba?
Clerk	Düz gidin, pasaport kontrolden önce, sağda ve solda iki tuvalet var. Pasaport kontrolden sonra iki tuvalet daha var.
Bahadır	Çok teşekkürler.
Clerk	Bir şey değil.
Bahadır	Taksiler nerede acaba?
Clerk	Kapıdan çıkın, yolu geçin, orada.

(Bahadır and Ülkü get into a taxi.)

Driver	Nereye, efendim?
Bahadır	Sultan Ahmet'e, lütfen. Sultan Ahmet uzak mı?
Driver	Biraz – 20 kilometre, 40 dakika falan.

Atatürk Havalimanı/ Istanbul Havalimanı

A	Geliş İskelesi	Arrivals Bridge
B	Vize Ofisi	Visa Office
C	Bagaj Alım Bantı	Incoming Baggage Band
D	Otel Rezervasyon	Hotel Reservation
E	Banka	Bank
F	Alış Veriş Merkezi	Shopping Centre
G	Yemek Alanları	Food Courts
H	Tuvaletler	Toilets
I	Kayıp Bagaj	Lost Luggage
J	Emanet	Luggage Custody
K	Oto Kiralama	Rent-A-Car
L	VIP Salonları	VIP Lounges
M	Transit Yolcu Bankosu	Transit Passenger Lounge
N	Merdivenler	Escalators

2 Read the dialogue again and look at the plan of İstanbul Havalimanı carefully. Were Bahadır and Ülkü given the correct directions for these places?

a Banka
b Tuvaletler
c Taksiler

2 IN SULTAN AHMET SQUARE

05.07 *Bahadır and Ülkü are in Sultan Ahmet Square. They ask for directions to some places of interest.*

1 What do they want to visit?

Ülkü	Afedersiniz, Topkapı Müzesi nerede acaba?
Passer-by	Efendim?
Ülkü	Topkapı Müzesi nerede acaba?
Passer-by	Özür dilerim, bilmiyorum.
(They ask someone else.)	
Ülkü	Afedersiniz, Topkapı nerede, acaba?
Passer-by	Düz gidin, köşeden sola dönün, tam karşıda.
Ülkü	Müzeler ne zaman açık?
Passer-by	Saat 9'dan 5'e kadar.
Ülkü	Teşekkürler.
Passer-by	Bir şey değil.
(They find the Topkapi Palace and go to the ticket office.)	
Bahadır	İki bilet, lütfen.
Receptionist	Buyrun. Çantaları buraya bırakın.
Bahadır	Teşekkürler. Harem nerede?
Receptionist	Düz gidin. Orada işaretler var.

2 When are the museums open?

3 Where is the Harem?

3 THE BLUE CRUISE

05.08 *Ülkü and Bahadır are at a tourist office in Bodrum, enquiring about cruises along the coast, known as 'Blue Cruises'.*

1 Which cruise do they decide to take?

Ülkü	Afedersiniz, Bodrum'dan Mavi Yolculuk var mı?
Clerk	Var.
Ülkü	Nereye var?
Clerk	Birincisi, Bodrum'dan Ören'e, Ören'den Körmen'e, Körmen'den
	tekrar Bodrum'a. İkincisi, Bodrum'dan Karaada'ya, Karaada'dan
	Cedre'ye, Cedre'den Ballısu'ya, Ballısu'dan Bodrum'a.
Ülkü	Aaa! Birinci güzel! Liman nerede?
Clerk	Sahilde, merkezde.
Ülkü	Teşekkürler.
Clerk	Rica ederim.

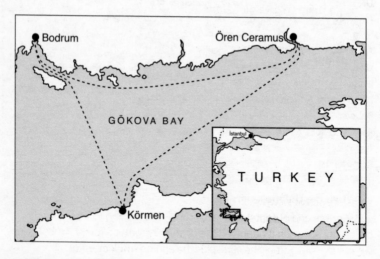

2 Where does the boat go from Bodrum?

3 Where is the port?

Language discovery

1 **Look at the words and polite phrases and complete the missing English. Reread the dialogues and try to guess the meanings from the texts. One has been done for you.**

a affedersiniz*   _____

b özür dilerim   *I'm sorry*

c acaba   _____

d efendim   _____

e bir şey değil   _____

f buyrun   _____

g rica ederim   _____

*In colloquial Turkish, **afedersiniz** has one **f**; in written Turkish it appears as **affedersiniz**.

2 **Practise the dialogues, using your name and the names of people you know.**

3 **Find these polite commands in the dialogues. Then practise using them to give directions.**

a sorun	*ask* (polite)
b gidin	*go* (polite)
c dönün	*turn/return* (polite)
d çıkın	*go out* (polite)
e geçin	*cross* (polite)
f bırakın	*leave* (polite)

Go further

1 VERBS, VERBS, VERBS

Verbs are action words such as *go, do, walk*. In Turkish, they generally come at the end of sentences. Verbs change according to who does the action and/or when it happens. The dictionary form of Turkish verbs is the stem, the main part of the verb, plus the ending **-mek** or **-mak**.

You will notice that some verbs have **-mek** endings while some have **-mak** endings. This is another example of vowel harmony. The ending is the one which rhymes best with the last vowel in that word, so it depends on the last vowel in the stem of the verb:

▶ **-mak** harmonises best with **a, ı, o, u**
▶ **-mek** harmonises best with **e, i, ö, ü**.

2 COMMANDS AND INSTRUCTIONS

In Turkish, you give informal commands such as **Git!** *Go!* by using the verb stem. You make the stem by taking the dictionary form of the verb and removing **-mek** or **-mak**. For example, the verb stem of **sormak** *to ask* is **sor** *ask!* and the verb stem of **dönmek** *to turn* is **dön** *turn!*

Here are some infinitives and their corresponding informal commands these are also called verb stems, main part of the verb:

sormak	to ask	**Sor!**	Ask!
gitmek	to go	**Git!**	Go!
geçmek	to cross	**Geç!**	Cross!
dönmek	to turn	**Dön!**	Turn!
çıkmak	to come out/go up	**Çık!**	Come out!
girmek	to enter	**Gir!**	Enter!
bırakmak	to leave	**Bırak!**	Leave!

3 FORMAL OR INFORMAL?

As you know, there are two ways of saying *you* (**sen** and **siz**) in Turkish, one formal and the other informal. You will therefore need to learn two ways of telling people what to do – one polite or formal, one friendly or informal. Here is the friendly or informal way:

Sor!	Ask!
Geç!	Cross!
Dön!	Turn!
Çık!	Come out!

To make the command more polite use the **siz** form. Take the verb stem (which is also the friendly form of command) and add **-in**, **-ın**, **-un** or **-ün**.

On warning signs and official notices you will see a third very formal form of command, using the following endings **-ınız**, **-iniz**, **-unuz**, **-ünüz**. You will probably never need to use this form yourself, but you do need to recognise it.

Vowel harmony yet again determines which ending to use. Choose the one which rhymes best with the last vowel in the word, following the rules of **i**-type vowel harmony:

▶ **-ın** and **-ınız** harmonises with/comes after **a, ı**
▶ **-un** and **-unuz** harmonises with/comes after **u, o**
▶ **-in** and **-iniz** harmonises with/comes after **i, e**
▶ **-ün** and **-ünüz** harmonises with/comes after **ü, ö**

Look at the table of polite and very formal commands. Notice the endings on the very formal commands.

Polite commands	Very formal commands
Sorun!	Sorunuz!
Geçin!	Geçiniz!
Dönün!	Dönünüz!

4 THE

There is no actual word for *the* in Turkish. But in some cases **-ı**, which has four variations (**-ı, -i, -u, -ü**), is used as a word ending to give the same meaning. These endings are principally used when the verb has a direct object (see next section). The **-i** ending follows **i**-type vowel harmony.

Işıkları geç.	*Pass the lights.*
Müzeyi geç.	*Pass the museum.*
Yolu geç.	*Cross the road.*
Otobüsü sür.	*Drive the bus.*

5 DIRECT OBJECTS

In Turkish, it is important to spot the direct object of a verb. A direct object is something or someone which is having an action carried out on it, as in the word *sun* in the sentence *Kate sees the sun*. There are direct objects in these commands:

Camiyi geç.	*Pass the mosque.*
Çayı iç.	*Drink the tea.*
Üzümü ye.	*Eat the grapes.*

In these examples, the direct objects are the things that are to be passed, drunk and eaten (*the mosque, the tea* and *the grapes*).

6 *THE* WITH DIRECT OBJECTS

Turkish does not usually distinguish between *a* and *the*. In the case of the direct object of a verb, however, Turkish does make a distinction: in this case it needs the equivalent of *the*. For direct objects, the Turkish equivalent of *the* is the ending **-i** (**-ı**, **-u**, **-ü**) or **-yi** (**-ı**, **-u**, **-ü**) if the noun ends in a vowel. As discussed in Unit 2, the equivalent of *a* is either **bir** or nothing.

Çay iç.	*Drink (some) tea.*
Bir çay iç.	*Drink a (one) tea.*
Çayı iç.	*Drink the tea.*
Araba sür.	*Drive a car.*
Bir araba sür.	*Drive a car.*
Arabayı sür.	*Drive the car.*

You use *the* in English to talk about specific items. Likewise in Turkish, you use the **-i** (**-ı**, **-u**, **-ü**) ending if the direct object is a specific item.

At this stage, don't worry about getting these endings right. People will understand you. Just try to notice them when you hear or see them.

Some commands do not have direct objects:

Git!	*Go!*
Çık!	*Come out/Get out!*
Dikkat et!	*Watch out!/Pay attention!/Be careful!*

---

7 WORD ORDER

Although Turkish word order is relatively free and flexible, it is best to follow the main principle that verbs go at the end of the sentence.

Git.	*Go.*
Sen git.	*You go.*
Sen müzeye git.	*You go to the museum.* (lit. *You museum to go.*)

The basic word order is subject (the person or thing performing the action) followed by object (the person or thing having the action done to it), and then the verb (the action word) at the end of the sentence. Remember this easily by **SOV** (**subject** – **object** – **verb**). Word order is described in more detail in Unit 7.

8 ENDINGS SHOWING POSITION OR MOVEMENT

-de, -da   *at/on/in*

Remember we covered the Turkish noun ending **-de** in Unit 4. It has two variations (**-de** and **-da**) and it means *at, on* or *in* with no movement.

-e, -a   *to*

The ending **-e**, which has two variations (**-e** and **-a**), means *to*, but indicates movement towards something. The endings follow the same principle of vowel harmony as **-de** and **-da**.

▶ **-a** harmonises best with **a, ı, o, u**
▶ **-e** harmonises best with **e, i, ö, ü**

Here are some examples:

İstanbul'a	*to Istanbul*
Türkiye'ye	*to Turkey*
Ankara'ya	*to Ankara*
müzeye	*to the museum*

Most proper nouns (names of places and people) have an apostrophe before the ending.

The next section explains the addition of **y**.

9 CONNECTING Y

In Turkish, you cannot put two vowels next to each other within a word as it makes pronunciation difficult. If a word ends in a vowel and the ending starts with a vowel, insert the consonant **-y-** between them, e.g., not **müzee** but **müzeye**. This makes the word more easily pronounceable.

10 -DEN, -DAN *FROM*

The ending **-den**, which has two variations (**-den** and **-dan**) means *from*, in the sense of movement away from something.

İngiltere'den	*from England*
Amerika'dan	*from America*
Saraydan camiye	*from the palace to the mosque*
Müzeden meydana	*from the museum to the square*

ⓘ Practice

1 Match the following traffic signs with what they mean.

a

1 *Sola dön.*

b

2 *Dur.*

c

3 *Düz git.*

d

4 *Sag˘a dön.*

2 Match the following questions and answers.
  a İçkiler kimden?
  b Kahveler senden mi?
  c Posta kartı kimden?
  d İstanbul nerede?
  e Ayasofya İstanbul'da mı?

  1 Evet, Sultan Ahmet'te.
  2 Vanessa'dan.
  3 Benden.
  4 Hayır, senden.
  5 Türkiye'de

3 Write down the meanings of the following Turkish phrases.

a Buyurun.

b Benden.

c Rahatsız etmeyin!

d Afedersiniz.

e Özür dilerim.

f Bilmiyorum.

g Teşekkürler.

h Rica ederim.

4 Here are some public signs with formal endings. Where would you see them?

a İtiniz.

b Çekiniz.

c Kart kullanınız.

d İstanbul'a Hoş Geldiniz.

e Yavaş sürünüz.

f Sağı takip ediniz.

1 on a door

2 on an escalator

3 on a door

4 on a road sign

5 on a public telephone

6 approaching Istanbul

5 05.09 **Look at the map showing distances from Istanbul to other cities in Turkey. Do the exercise first, then listen for the answers. Practise repeating the questions and answers. For help with the numbers, see Units 2 and 3.**

a İstanbul'dan Ankara'ya kaç km?

b İstanbul'dan Bodrum'a kaç km?

c İstanbul'dan Çanakkale'ye kaç km?

d İstanbul'dan Safranbolu'ya kaç km?

e İstanbul'dan Pamukkale'ye kaç km?

f İstanbul'dan Marmaris'e kaç km?

g İstanbul'dan Göreme'ye kaç km?

h İstanbul'dan İzmir'e kaç km?

i İstanbul'dan Trabzon'a kaç km?

j İstanbul'dan Fethiye'ye kaç km?

 6 05.10 **Listen to the audio of the routes of the Blue Cruises and stops while looking at the map. Then put the necessary endings on the place names, e.g., -den, -dan** (*from*), **-e, -a** (*to*).

a	Birinci gün	Marmaris – Çiftlik
b	İkinci gün	Çiftlik – Bozukkale
c	Üçüncü gün	Bozukkale – Aktur – Datça
d	Dördüncü gün	Datça – Knidos
e	Beşinci gün	Knidos – Bodrum

Note: **d** becomes **t** after these consonants: **ç, f, h, k, p, s, ş, t**. But don't worry too much about consonant changes at this stage.

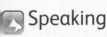

Speaking

05.11 **Listen to the conversation. Then practise role playing each part.**

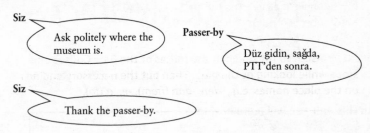

Siz

Ask politely where the museum is.

Passer-by

Düz gidin, sağda, PTT'den sonra.

Siz

Thank the passer-by.

Test yourself

05.12 **Listen and answer the following questions orally or in writing.**

1 Ask for directions to the bank.

2 Ask where the taxis are.

3 Tell a taxi driver to go straight on and turn right at the corner.

4 Ask when the museum is open.

5 Ask for two tickets.

If you get any wrong, go back through the unit and have another look before moving on to the next unit.

SELF CHECK	
	I CAN. . .
●	. . . ask for and give directions.
●	. . . get around a new place.
●	. . . ask what something means.
●	. . . ask when something is open.

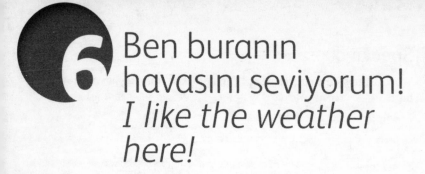

6 Ben buranın havasını seviyorum!
I like the weather here!

In this unit you will learn how to:
▶ *talk about the weather.*
▶ *name directions on the compass.*
▶ *compare months and seasons.*
▶ *talk about your likes and dislikes.*

CEFR: *(A2) Can understand sentences and frequently used expressions related to local geography, climate. Can talk to people about the weather, compare months and seasons and express likes and dislikes.*

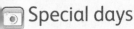 Special days

The followings are all important dates in the Turkish calendar. Why not put the dates, days of the week and months of the year in your diary in Turkish?

Bayramlar *Fixed public holidays*

> **TIP**
>
> **Bayram** is the Turkish word for a nationally celebrated festival or holiday, applicable to both national (i.e., secular) and religious celebrations. The yearly timing of **Bayramlar** is different for national and religious holidays.

National Bayramlar

1 Ocak	Yılbaşı	*New Year's Day, 1st January*
23 Nisan	Çocuk Bayramı	*National Sovereignty and Children's Day, 23rd April*
1 Mayıs	Emek ve Dayanışma Günü	*Labour and Solidarity Day, 1st May*
19 Mayıs	Gençlik ve Spor Bayramı	*Atatürk Commemoration and Youth and Sports Day, 19th May*
30 Ağustos	Zafer Bayramı	*Victory Day, 30th August*
29 Ekim	Cumhuriyet Bayramı	*Republic Day, 29th October*

Religious Bayramlar (Moveable Islamic public holidays)

| **Ramazan/Şeker Bayramı** | *Ramadan/End of the Fast* |
| **Kurban Bayramı** | *Helping the Poor* |

Non-holiday celebrations

| **Mayısın 2'nci pazar günü** | *Mother's Day* |
| **Anneler Günü** | |

During the month of **Ramazan** (*Ramadan*), practising Muslims do not eat or drink between **şafak** (*sunrise*) and **gün batımı** (*sunset*) (local time is used). In traditional areas, restaurants do not open until sunset, but in tourist areas, places to eat and drink are open as usual during daylight hours even during **Ramazan**. If you are not Muslim, don't worry – you are not expected to **oruç tutmak** (*fast*).

However, as a sign of respect, you may decide not to eat or drink too overtly. At sunset during **Ramazan**, there is an air of celebration as people come together to break their fast. The dates of **Ramazan** change each year, as they are set by the lunar calendar. At the end of the fasting month, there is a national holiday, **Şeker Bayramı**, which is a time of celebration when families get together. The standard greeting during the **Ramazan** and **Kurban** holidays is **İyi Bayramlar!** (*Have a good Bayram!*)

1   Turkish and English ways of writing dates are given above. How do they differ?
2   What do you think Kurban Bayramı might involve?

Vocabulary builder

TRAVEL

 06.01 **Listen and repeat. Then complete the missing parts of the Turkish sentences.**

Temmuzda, _____ _____ Antalya.	*In July, Antalya is the hottest.*
Yazın güneyde hiç yağmur yok.	*There is no rain in the summer in the south.*
Hava hep _____.	*The weather is sunny all the time.*
Kırlarda kır çiçekleri çok çeşitli ve güzeldir.	*In the countryside, there is a variety of beautiful wild flowers.*

YÖNLER PUSULA *POINTS OF THE COMPASS*

 06.02 **Listen, then repeat.**

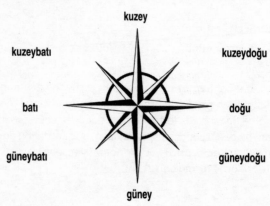

6 Ben buranın havasını seviyorum! I like the weather here!

DÖRT MEVSİM *THE FOUR SEASONS*

 06.03 **Listen, then repeat.**

ilkbahar	spring
yaz	summer
sonbahar	autumn
kış	winter

To say *in spring*, and so on:

ilkbaharda	in spring
yazın	in summer
sonbaharda	in autumn
kışın	in winter

AYLAR *THE MONTHS OF THE YEAR*

 06.04 **Listen, then repeat.**

ocak	*January*	temmuz	*July*
şubat	*February*	ağustos	*August*
mart	*March*	eylül	*September*
nisan	*April*	ekim	*October*
mayıs	*May*	kasım	*November*
haziran	*June*	aralık	*December*

To say *in June*, and so on, you add the **-de** or **-da** ending, according to vowel harmony:

haziranda   *in June*

HAFTANIN GÜNLERI *THE DAYS OF THE WEEK*

 06.05 **Listen, then repeat.**

pazar (günü)	*(on) Sunday*
pazartesi (günü)	*(on) Monday*
salı (günü)	*(on) Tuesday*
çarşamba (günü)	*(on) Wednesday*
perşembe (günü)	*(on) Thursday*
cuma (günü)	*(on) Friday*
cumartesi (günü)	*(on) Saturday*

NEW EXPRESSIONS

Listen to the words and phrases you will hear in the dialogues. Practise listening and saying the expressions until you feel you have learned them.

Dialogue 1 At a travel agency

 06.06

sıcak	*hot*
ılık	*warm*
seviyoruz	*we like/love*
yağmur	*rain*
sevmiyoruz	*we do not like/love*
çocuklar	*children*
deniz	*sea*
kum	*sand*
en	*the most (the-est)*
en sıcak	*hottest*
hava	*weather*
hiç	*(not) at all, never*
hep	*all*
güneşli	*sunny*
daha çok	*mostly*
daha	*more (-er)*
sonra	*then*
gökkuşağı	*rainbow*
kır	*countryside/wild*
kır çiçekleri	*wild flowers*
çeşitli	*various*
gün	*day*
uçak	*aeroplane/flight*
yer	*place/seat*
kaç kişilik?	*for how many people?*

6 Ben buranın havasını seviyorum! I like the weather here!

Dialogue 2 We like different things

06.07

futbol	*football*
basketbol	*basketball*
voleybol	*volleyball*
tenis	*tennis*
dans	*dance*
günlük	*daily (day)*
gezi	*trip/journey*
yağmursuz	*without rain*
rüzgarsız	*without wind*
annemler	*my parents* (lit. *my mother*)
özellikle	*especially*
harabe	*ruin*
gezmek	*to travel/to have a trip*
yemek yemek	*to eat food*
keyifli	*joyous, pleasurable, enjoyable*
orada	*there*
gölge	*shade*
dondurma	*ice cream*
çikolatalı	*chocolate flavoured/with chocolate*
sade	*plain/vanilla flavoured*
meyveli	*fruit flavoured/with fruit*
limonlu	*lemon flavoured*
karışık	*mixed*
bana	*for me*

Dialogues

**Read the introduction and the gist question for each conversation.
Then listen or read the conversation and answer the questions.**

1 AT A TRAVEL AGENCY

 06.08 *Anne and her partner are at a travel agency looking for a suitable holiday destination.*

1 Is Antalya hot in July?

Anne	Türkiye'de nereleri sıcak?
Memur	Güney, ağustos ve temmuzda çok sıcak. İlkbaharda ılık, haziranda sıcak.
Anne	Biz çok sıcak seviyoruz. Yağmur sevmiyoruz. Çocuklar da denizi ve kumu seviyor.

(The travel agent looks at the average temperatures for various places in Turkey.)

Memur	Temmuzda Alanya 26°C, Antalya 28°C, Bodrum 27°C, Fethiye 27°C, İstanbul 23°C. Temmuzda, en sıcak Antalya. Yazın güneyde hiç yağmur yok. Hava hep güneşli. İlkbaharda daha çok bahar yağmurları ve sonra da gökkuşağı vardır. Kırlarda kır çiçekleri çok çeşitli ve güzeldir.
Anne	Evet. Antalya'ya hangi günler uçak var?

*(The travel agent looks at the computer (**bilgisayar**) flight timetable.)*

Memur	Pazartesi, çarşamba, cuma günde bir uçak. Cumartesi ve pazar günde iki uçak var.
Anne	5 mayıs pazar günü yer var mı?
Memur	Evet, var. Kaç kişilik?

2 Of the places mentioned, which is coolest?

3 Which days are there flights to Antalya?

06.09 *Some young people are sitting at a seaside café in the shade of a willow tree.*

1 What are they talking about?

Cem	Ben ve Gökhan futbol, basketbol, voleybol ve tenis seviyoruz.
Gökhan	Ama en çok futbolu.
Vanessa	Biz denizi ve dansı, günlük gezileri seviyoruz. Yağmursuz ve rüzgarsız ne güzel bir gün!
Cem	Annemler de günlük gezileri, özellikle harabeleri gezmeyi seviyor. Restoranlarda yemek yemek çok keyifli. *(To a friend standing in the sun)* Orada durma, çok güneş var, gölgeye gel.
(He calls out to the waiter to order some ice cream.)	
	Garson, bana bir çikolatalı dondurma.
(They all order different flavours of ice cream.)	
Vanessa	Bana sade dondurma.
Cem	Bana meyveli.
Çiğdem	Bana limonlu.
Gökhan	Bana da karışık.
Garson	Tamam, efendim.

2 What does each of the friends like?

3 What ice cream flavours sound like English?

 # Language discovery

1 Answer these questions about the dialogues. Use Turkish where possible.

   a How does Anne say *And (the) children love the sea and the sand*?

   b What does the travel agent say about the wild flowers?

   c What kinds of ice cream are mentioned?

2 Practise the dialogues, using your name and the names of people you know.

Go further

1 FORMAL -DIR (-DİR, -DUR, -DÜR)

Match the Turkish sentences with their English equivalents.

a Gökkuşağı vardır.

b Kır çiçekleri çok çeşitli ve güzeldir.

c Türkiye'de dört mevsim vardır.

d Yazlar yağmursuzdur.

1 There is no rain in the summer.

2 There is a rainbow.

3 The wild flowers are varied and beautiful.

4 There are four seasons in Turkey.

You have already seen that there is no equivalent of the English word *is*. The Turkish sentence **Ev kırmızı** means *The house is red*, but the literal translation is *House red*.

Notice that these sentences are very formal:

Durmak yasaktır. *Stopping is forbidden.*

Geçmek yasaktır. *Crossing/passing is forbidden.*

Türklerin dili Türkçe'dir. *The language of Turks is Turkish.*

You would not commonly use the **-dir** ending in conversation, but you need to recognise it when you see it, usually on official notices, in official documents and in newspaper articles.

You will also notice that **d** changes to **t** after **k**. At this stage it is not important to remember to make this change but it is important to recognise it when you see it. (Also see Unit 9.)

Another use of **-dir** is for describing unchanging facts:

Güney Türkiye'de yazlar çok sıcaktır. *In southern Turkey, summers are very hot.*

Notice the **-dır** (**-dir**, **-dur**, **-dür**) endings in Dialogue 2.

2 MORE ABOUT VERB ENDINGS

In Turkish, certain verbs take certain endings. Good bilingual dictionaries give these endings next to the verb. When you look up a new verb, look to see if there is an ending shown as well.

For example, in a good dictionary you would see:

> **gelmek, -ir** 1. *to come.* 2. /a/ *to come to.* 3. **/dan/** *to come from* 4. /a/ *to come into;* *to come in, etc.*
>
> *come,* f. 1. **gelmek -e erişmek, - ulaşmak**. 2. **-e varmak, -i keşfetmek**
>
> **sevmek** /ı/ 1. *to love; to like.* 2. *to fondle, caress.*
>
> **Sev beni, seveyim seni.** proverb *You scratch my back and I'll scratch yours.*
>
> *love,* f. **sevmek, aşık olmak**. i 1. **sevgi**. 2. *aşk fall/be in love with* **-e aşık olmak**.
>
> **f = fiil** = *verb*
>
> **i = isim** = *noun*

Notice which ending **sevmek** (*to love*) takes.

Biz yazı seviyoruz.	*We love summers (i.e., We love the summer).*
Biz güneşi çok seviyoruz.	*We love the sun.*
Biz yağmuru sevmiyoruz.	*We do not like/love the rain.*

3 COMPARATIVES AND SUPERLATIVES

In English there are two ways to say *more* and *most*: with short words -*er* or -*est* are added (*nicer, nicest*), and with longer words *more* and *most* are used (*more beautiful, most beautiful*).

Look at the table. Can you figure out on your own how to make comparatives and superlatives in Turkish? Then find the missing forms in the dialogues and complete the table.

Adjective	Comparative	Superlative
sıcak	daha sıcak	_____
çok	daha çok	en çok
ılık	_____	en ılık
serin	_____	en serin
soğuk	daha soğuk	_____

daha *more (-er)*

For a simple comparative, add the word **daha** before the adjective:

daha sıcak	*hotter/warmer*
Bugün hava daha sıcak.	*The weather is hotter today. (lit. Today weather hotter.)*
daha güzel	*more beautiful*

Then, to compare one thing to another you add the ending **-den**, **-dan**, **-ten**, **-tan** to the adjective:

Bugün hava dünden daha sıcak.	*Today the weather is warmer than yesterday.*
Temmuzda hava hazirandan daha sıcak.	*The weather in July is warmer than in June. (lit. In July weather than June hotter.)*

en	*the most (the -est)*

For a superlative, add the word **en** before the adjective:

en sıcak	*the warmest (hottest)*
Rize en yağmurlu.	*Rize is the rainiest. (lit. Rize most rainy/rainiest.)*

4 MAKING ADJECTIVES USING THE ENDING -LI (-Lİ, -LU, -LÜ)

Add the ending **-li** (**-lı**, **-lu**, **-lü**) to a noun to make an adjective.

güneş	*sun*	**güneşli**	*sunny*

Find the words in the dialogues that have **-li** (**-lı**, **-lu**, **-lü**) endings. What do you think the ending means?*

*The ending **-li** (**-lı**, **-lu**, **-lü**) can be translated as *with*.

Remember that **Hava nasıl?** means *What is the weather like?* (lit. *weather how?*)

5 THE ENDING -SİZ (-SIZ, -SUZ, -SÜZ)

The ending **-siz** means *without*. It is the opposite of the **-li** ending, which means *with*. You add both to the end of nouns to make adjectives.

Look at the **-siz** (**-sız**, **-suz**, **-süz**) endings. What determines the vowel changes in each?

güneşsiz	*without sun*
bulutsuz	*without cloud*
yağmursuz	*without rain*
karsız	*without snow*
üzümsüz	*without grapes*

This is another example of the **i**-type vowel harmony. Now you know how to make two different adjectives from each noun!

6 THE ENDING -ME, -MA

Find the sentence with the **-ma** ending in the second dialogue. Can you guess what it means?

Infinitive	Informal negative command	Polite negative command	Formal negative command
durmak *to stop*	**durma** *don't stop*	**durmayın**	**durmayınız**
geçmek *to cross*	**geçme** *don't cross*	**geçmeyin**	**geçmeyiniz**

To tell people not to do things, add **-me** or **-ma** to the end of an informal command. For formal negative commands, you then add **-in** or **-iniz** to the informal negative (**-iniz** is very formal). Study the above examples.

Look at the following examples. Can you figure out the difference between the **-me**, **-ma** negative endings and the negative **değil**?

durma	*don't stop, don't stand*	**güneşli değil**	*not sunny*
geçme	*don't pass, don't cross*	**dondurma değil**	*not ice cream*
yeme	*don't eat*	**ilkbahar değil**	*not spring*
sevme	*don't like, don't love*	**soğuk değil**	*not cold*

The ending **-me** or **-ma** comes after verbs, not after nouns or adjectives. **Değil** is a separate word used to make adjectives or nouns negative.

7 CAPITAL LETTERS

Unlike English, Turkish does not use capital letters for the days of the week and months of the year unless they are important dates or special days.

For example, in the sentence **Her pazar çok uyuyorum** (*Every Sunday I sleep a lot*) you can see that there is no capital letter for **pazar**. However, when writing about *1st May*, which is the Spring Festival, a capital letter is used: **1 Mayıs**.

1 Mayıs Emek ve Dayanışma Günü'dür.   *1st May is Labour and Solidarity Day.*

8 DATES

Writing or saying dates is very easy. Simply say the number followed by the month:

bir mayıs   *1st May*

yirmi iki şubat   *22nd February*

Years are read just like a number, so the year 2222 would be **iki bin iki yüz yirmi iki** (*two thousand two hundred twenty-two*).

9 ANNEMLER *MY MOTHER AND FATHER*

Anne means *mother*. **Annem** means *my mother*. **Annemler** is the plural form, and it means *my mother and my father*.

> Notice that the plural *mother and father* derives from the word for *mother*; there is no separate word meaning *parent*.

Ayşeler means *Ayşe and her family*.

This is similar to *the Browns* in English, but in Turkish, first names or titles are used instead of surnames. This practice is informal and very common.

Practice

1 06.10 **Look at the map of Turkey and write down where these places are, using the points of the compass. The first one has been done for you. Then repeat what the speaker says on the audio.**

a İzmir nerede? _____Batıda*_____
b İstanbul nerede? _____
c Ankara nerede? _____
d Van nerede? _____
e Bodrum nerede? _____
f Samsun nerede? _____
g Mersin nerede? _____
h Alanya nerede? _____
i Marmaris nerede? _____

*Remember to add the ending.

2 Match the words with the corresponding pictures. Then write the opposites by adding *-siz* endings.

a güneşli
b bulutlu
c yağmurlu
d karlı
e sisli
f sıcak
g soğuk

3 Can you work out the answer to this puzzle?

Ali, Betül'den daha uzun boylu, ama Ali Can'dan daha kısa boylu. Dursun, Betül'den daha kısa boylu. En kısa boylu kim?

4 Fill in the blanks to complete the months of the year:

a a _ us _ _ s
b _ yl _ l
c _ _ i _

d h _ zi _ _ n
e te _ _ u _
f _ ub _ t

5 Match the Turkish words with their English equivalents.

a	spor	**1**	dance
b	futbol	**2**	volleyball
c	basketbol	**3**	basketball
d	voleybol	**4**	tennis
e	tenis	**5**	sport
f	dans	**6**	football

Pronunciation

06.11 Try another Turkish tongue twister.

Şu köşe yaz köşesi, bu köşe kış köşesi. *That corner (of the room, garden, etc.) is the summer corner, this corner is the winter corner.*

Speaking

06.12 Listen to the conversation. Then practise role playing each part.

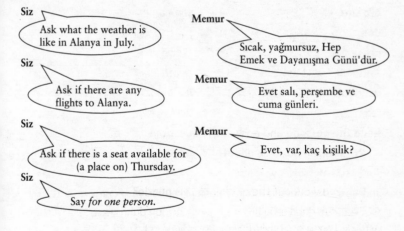

Siz — Ask what the weather is like in Alanya in July.

Memur — Sıcak, yağmursuz, Hep Emek ve Dayanışma Günü'dür.

Siz — Ask if there are any flights to Alanya.

Memur — Evet salı, perşembe ve cuma günleri.

Siz — Ask if there is a seat available for (a place on) Thursday.

Memur — Evet, var, kaç kişilik?

Siz — Say *for one person.*

Reading and writing

Look at the words; then listen to the words and repeat them.

iklim	*climate*
bölge	*region*
farklı	*different*
Akdeniz	*Mediterranean*
Ege	*Aegean*
Marmara	*Marmara* (the sea and region)
kurak	*dry*
yüksek	*high*
dağ	*mountain*
deniz kenarları	*seaside*
ortalama	*average*
Karadeniz	*the Black Sea*
serin	*cool*
ara sıra	*sometimes*
don	*frost*
arasında	*between*
Anadolu	*Anatolia*
uzundur	*it is long*
iken	*while/when*

Read the passage and answer the questions.

1 **What is the passage about?**

Türkiye'de mevsimler ve iklim

Türkiye'de dört mevsim vardır ve bunlar ilkbahar, yaz, sonbahar, kıştır. İklim de her bölgede çok farklıdır.

Akdeniz, Ege ve Marmara'da yazlar sıcak ve kurak, kışlar ılık ve yağmurludur. Çok yüksek dağlarda kar vardır. Türkiye'de deniz kenarları daha ılıktır. İstanbul ve Marmara'da kışlar ortalama 4°C, yazlar 27°C.

Karadeniz'de yazlar sıcaktır. Kışlar güneyden daha serindir. Ara sıra don ve her mevsimde kar vardır. Yazlar 23°C ve kışlar 7°C'dır. En çok yağmur Rize'dedir.

Orta Anadolu'da gece ve gündüz arasında sıcaklık çok farklıdır. Yazlar daha az sıcaktır. Ortalama sıcaklık yazlarda 23°C, kışlarda –2°C. Güneydoğu Anadolu'da yazlar çok sıcak, kışlar daha az soğuktur.

Doğu Anadolu'da kışlar çok soğuk, karlı ve uzundur. Yazlar yağmursuzdur. Türkiye'de en soğuk yerler kuzey doğudur.

Güneyde kumda iken Toroslar'da kar vardır.

2 Is the weather the same everywhere all year?

3 Now write a similar short passage about the weather in your country. Compare the weather in Turkey.

Test yourself

06.14 Listen and answer the following questions orally or in writing.

1 Say there is no rain in summer.

2 Say that it rains in spring.

3 Say that July is hotter than February.

4 Say you like dancing and volleyball the most.

5 Ask what day there are flights to Bodrum.

SELF CHECK

I CAN...
. . . talk about the weather.
. . . name directions on the compass.
. . . compare months and seasons.
. . . talk about my likes and dislikes.

Kendimizi ve insanları tanımlam *Describing ourselves and people*

In this unit you will learn how to:
▶ *talk about yourself.*
▶ *ask people about themselves.*
▶ *describe yourself and other people.*
▶ *ask where people are from.*

CEFR: *(A2) Can talk about oneself, describe other people and ask and answer questions about personal details. Can address people using an appropriate level of formality.*

Addressing people

In Turkey, only people who are very close call each other by their first names (see Unit 1), and then only if they are more or less the same age. In the case of an age gap, the younger person will use an additional polite address form when speaking to the older person. For an older woman this would be **Hanım**, as in **Gül Hanım**, or just **Hanımefendi**. For an older man, this would be **Bey** as in **Ahmet Bey** or just **Beyefendi**. To address an older person who also has a professional title, the title comes first, as in **Doktor Bahadır Bey** or just **Doktor Bey**, **Profesör Hanım**, **Garson Bey**. **Hanım** is the equivalent of *Ms*, *Miss* or *Mrs* and **Bey** is the equivalent of *Mr*. The important thing to remember, though, is that they are used with the first name, not the surname.

> **TIPS**
> Surnames were only introduced in 1934 during Atatürk's modernization reforms.

Social closeness is expressed by using the words for family relations. If one person calls another **amca** (*uncle*), **abla** (*elder sister*), **abi** (*elder brother*) or **teyze** (*auntie*), it does not necessarily mean that they are related. In Dialogue 3, you will hear Ülkü refer to her friend as **Gonca Abla**, which shows affection and respect for an older woman. The same family terms are used to indicate that there is no sexual motive when talking to someone of the opposite sex, that one's intentions are purely innocent and family-like. It is quite acceptable for a young man sitting on a bus to call over to an older woman **Abla gel otur** (*Older/big sister, come and sit down*). You could add to this list **anne** (*mother*), **nene** (*grandmother*), **baba** (*father*) and **dede** (*grandfather*).

Make two lists of words from the above text: one for words used for men and one for words used for women.

Vocabulary builder

DİLLER *LANGUAGES*

07.01 Listen and repeat the names of languages you will hear. Then complete the missing parts of the Turkish.

Türkçe*	Turkish (language)
_____ca	German (language)
Fransızca	French (language)
_____ca	Spanish (language)
İtalyanca	Italian (language)
_____ca	Bulgarian (language)

*See Language discovery for information on **-ce** or **-ca** endings.

Türkiyeli'yim.	I'm from Turkey.
İngetereli'yim.	I'm from England.

NEW EXPRESSIONS

Listen to the words and phrases you will hear in the dialogues. Practise listening and saying the expressions until you feel you have learned them.

Dialogue 1 Where are you from?

07.02

Nerelisin?	*Where are you from?*
eşim	*my wife/my husband (my spouse)*
biliyorum	*I know*
kızımız	*our daughter*
seviyorum	*I like*
gerçekten	*really*
ilginç	*interesting*
tatil	*holiday*
keyifli	*enjoyable*
şans	*chance/luck*
samimi	*friendly/sincere*
dürüst	*honest*
Haklısınız.	*You are right.*

Dialogue 2 Are you Turkish?

07.03

meslekler/iş	*jobs*
manken/model	*model*
öğrenci	*student*
doktor	*doctor*
mühendis	*engineer*
futbolcu	*footballer*
hostes	*flight attendant*
fotoğrafçı	*photograph*
akıllı	*clever*
çalışkan	*hard working*
evli	*married*
nişanlı	*engaged*
bekar	*single*
henüz	*only*
X yaşındayım.	*I'm x years old.*
nişanlın	*your fiancé*
yakışıklı	*handsome*
uzun boylu	*tall*
esmer	*dark/olive skinned*
siyah saçlı	*black haired*
siyah gözlü	*dark-brown eyed (lit. black eyed)*
tabii	*of course*
bence	*in my opinion*

7 kendimizi ve insanlahı tanımlamı Describing ourselves and people

| insan | person |
| arkadaş | friend |

See Language discovery for more **-lı** (**-li -lu**, **-lü**) endings.

Dialogue 3 How are you?

07.04

| benim | it's me |
| canım | my dear |

Dialogue 4 Hello?

07.05

| Alo? | Hello? |

Dialogues

Read the introduction and the gist question for each conversation. Then listen or read the conversation and answer the questions.

1 WHERE ARE YOU FROM?

07.06 *Two passengers on a flight to Istanbul strike up a conversation.*

1 Where are the two people from?

Kadın	Merhaba.
Erkek	Merhaba.
Kadın	Nerelisin?
Erkek	Leeds'liyim. Ya siz nerelisiniz?
Kadın	Ben Almanım. Bonn'luyum.
Erkek	Ben İngilizim ama eşim Türk, İstanbullu. *(The man holds up a book.)* Bu kitap Türkçe öğrenmek için, *Teach Yourself Turkish*. Ben hem Türkçe hem de Almanca, Fransızca, İspanyolca, İtalyanca ve biraz da Bulgarca biliyorum. Türkleri, Türkçe'yi ve Türkiye'yi çok seviyorum. Kızımız Vanessa da Türkçe biliyor.
Kadın	Gerçekten mi? Çok ilginç.
Erkek	Tatillerde Türkiye'ye gitmek çok keyifli. Biz çok şanslıyız. Türkler çok samimi ve dürüst, değil mi?
Kadın	Evet, haklısınız.

2 How many languages does the man speak?

2 ARE YOU TURKISH?

 *07.07 Two young women are sitting next to each other on the **otobüs** (coach/bus) to Ankara. They introduce themselves and begin to chat.*

1 Where are the women from?

Susie	Merhaba, ben Susie. Ya sen?
Ayda	Ben Ayda.
Susie	Türk müsün?
Ayda	Evet. Ya sen? Amerikalı mısın?
Susie	Hayır. İngilizim. Londralı'yım.
Ayda	Manken misin?
Susie	Hayır, öğrenciyim. Ya sen?
Ayda	Ben doktorum.
Susie	Çok akıllısın.
Ayda	Çok akıllı değilim ama çok çalışkanım.
Susie	Evli misin?
Ayda	Hayır, nişanlıyım. Sen?
Susie	Ben bekarım, henüz 23 yaşındayım. Nişanlın yakışıklı mı?

(Ayda takes out a photograph of her fiancé from her wallet and describes him to Susie.)

Ayda	Cem uzun boylu, esmer, siyah saçlı, siyah gözlü ve tabii bence çok yakışıklı. Çok akıllı ve iyi bir insan. Mühendis ve biz çok iyi arkadaşız.

2 Who is a model?

3 What is Cem like?

3 HOW ARE YOU?

 07.08 Ülkü phones her good friend Gonca.

1 What name does Ülkü call Gonca?

Ülkü	Alo!
Gonca	Alo. Ülkü, sen misin?
Ülkü	Benim. Gonca Abla, siz misiniz?
Gonca	Benim canım. Nasılsın?
Ülkü	Teşekkür ederim, iyiyim. Siz nasılsınız?
Gonca	Ben de iyiyim.

2 How is Ülkü?

3 How is Gonca?

4 HELLO?

07.09 *Şafak phones his cousin Banu.*

1 Do they speak formally or informally? How do you know?

Banu	Alo?
Şafak	Merhaba, Banu, ben Şafak.
Banu	Merhaba Şafak. Nasılsın?
Şafak	İyiyim.

2 How is Şafak?

Language discovery

1 Answer these questions about Dialogue 1. Use Turkish where possible.

  a How does the woman say *I'm German*?

  b How does the man say *My wife is from Istanbul*?

  c How does the woman say *Yes, you are right*?

2 Find the following word endings in Dialogues 1 and 2. What words come before them? These are personal endings/verb *to be*.

  a _____sin

  b _____im

  c _____siniz

  d _____ım

  e _____um

  f _____ız

  g _____sınız

  h _____sün

  i _____sın

  j What determines the vowel changes?

3 Practise the dialogues, using your name and the names of people you know.

Go further

1 MORE ON ENDINGS

As you have seen, the closest Turkish equivalents to the English verb *to be* are the endings **-im**, **-sin**, **-iz**, **-siniz** and **-ler** (**-lar**). **O** is a separate word and does not take the verb *to be* ending.

Singular	Plural
benim *I am*	**biziz** *we are*
sensin *you are* (informal)	**sizsiniz** *you are* (formal/plural)
o *he/she/it is*	**onlar** *they are*

Once you have learned these endings, you can add them to adjectives, nouns and pronouns you already know to make a huge number of new sentences very easily and quickly.

Türkler çok dürüst.	*Turks are very honest.*
Biz çok iyi arkadaşız.	*We are very good friends.*
O doctor.	*He/She is a doctor.*
Benim.	*It's me.*

2 NATIONALITIES

Here are some examples of sentences about nationality with the appropriate endings, showing vowel harmony:

ben	İngilizim	İspanyolum	Türküm	Almanım
sen	İngilizsin	İspanyolsun	Türksün	Almansın
o	İngiliz*	İspanyol*	Türk*	Alman*
biz	İngiliziz	İspanyoluz	Türküz	Almanız
siz	İngilizsiniz	İspanyolsunuz	Türksünüz	Almansınız
onlar	İngiliz(ler)	İspanyol(lar)	Türk(ler)	Alman(lar)

*Note that there is no ending on the **o** form. Note also that the **-ler** is shown in parentheses; this is because it is usually left out.

Most adjectives follow the pattern above, but the letter **y** is added when the root word ends in a vowel and the personal ending starts with a vowel. This 'buffer **y**' makes the word easier to pronounce.

Amerikalı'yız.   *We are American.*

Amerikalı'yım.   *I am American.*

3 LANGUAGES

The endings **-ce** and **-ca** are used to denote languages:

İngiliz	English (nationality)	**İngilizce**	*English* (language)
Alman	*German* (nationality)	**Almanca**	*German* (language)
Fransız	*French* (nationality)	**Fransızca**	*French* (language)
Türk	*Turkish* (nationality)	**Türkçe**	*Turkish* (language)
Rus	*Russian* (nationality)	**Rusça**	*Russian* (language)

For more nationalities and languages, see the Glossary.

4 PROFESSIONS

You have already seen how the equivalent of the verb *to be* is used with adjectives such as nationalities. The endings can also be used with nouns. In Dialogue 2, you saw the endings of the verb *to be* used with the names of jobs.

Here is an example of a noun **sekreter** (*secretary*) with the personal endings added:

Sekreterim.   *I am a secretary.*

Sekretersin.   *You are a secretary.*

Sekreter.   *He/She is a secretary.*

Sekreteriz.   *We are secretaries.*

Sekretersiniz.   *You are secretaries.*

Sekreterler.   *They are secretaries.*

The following table provides examples of some other jobs to show vowel harmony:

	öğretmen	doktor	profesör	bakkal
	teacher	*doctor*	*professor*	*grocer*
ben	Öğretmenim.	Doktorum.	Profesörüm.	Bakkalım.
sen	Öğretmensin.	Doktorsun.	Profesörsün.	Bakkalsın.
o	Öğretmen.	Doktor.	Profesör.	Bakkal.
biz	Öğretmeniz.	Doktoruz.	Profesörüz.	Bakkalız.
siz	Öğretmensiniz.	Doktorsunuz.	Profesörsünüz.	Bakkalsınız.
onlar	Öğretmen(ler).	Doktor(lar).	Profesör(ler).	Bakkal(lar).

In Turkish, you will come across simple verbless sentences, e.g., **Doktor.** (*He/She is a doctor.*), **Çalışkan.** (*He/She is hard working*). As you can see in the table, *he/she/it* do not take any endings.

The actual personal pronouns (**ben**, **sen**, etc.) can be used when you want to emphasise the point. For example, **Ben öğ, retmenim** (*I am a teacher not you*).

Otherwise, just using the verb *to be* endings (**-im**, **-sin**, etc.) is enough, as in **Öğretmenim** (*I'm a teacher*).

You may be wondering how you will know whether **Öğretmen** means *He is a teacher* or *She is a teacher*, but this will usually be clear from the context – you will normally know who you are having a conversation about! If you need to clarify, you can ask who the teacher is. **Kim öğretmen?** (*Who is the teacher?*)

5 CANIM *MY DEAR*

Canım means literally *my soul*, but it is used as an affectionate term to mean *my dear*. You heard Gonca refer to Ülkü as **canım** in Dialogue 3. Another way of expressing the same feeling is to add the ending **-cığım** after a loved one's name or title. For example, **canım Cemciğim** (*my dear, dear Cem*), **anneciğim** (*my dear mother*).

6 BEN/BENIM/-M/-IM *I AM/MY*

When added to nouns and adjectives the ending **-m** can mean *my* if the word finishes with a vowel as in **kahve** + **m/kahvem** (*my coffee*) and if the word finishes with a consonant as in **ben** + **im/benim** or as in **can** + **ım/canım -im** (**-ım**, **-um**, **-üm**).

A: **Tık tık.**	*Knock knock.*
B: **Kim o?**	*Who is it/that?*
A: **Benim, canım.**	*It's me, my dear.*

When a mother cuddles her child she might say **canım benim** or **benim canım** *my dear*.

Ben öğretmenim.	*I am a teacher.*
Benim öğretmenim.	*My teacher.*
Ben güzelim.	*I am beautiful.*
Benim güzelim.	*My beauty.*

7 NEGATIVES WITH *TO BE*

You have already learned that **değil** means *not*. Study the following pattern to see where the negative *to be* equivalent comes.

değil-im	**Ben bakkal değilim.**	*I am not a grocer.*
değil-sin	**Sen bakkal değilsin.**	*You are not a grocer.*
değil	**O bakkal değil.**	*He/She is not a grocer.*
değil-iz	**Biz bakkal değiliz.**	*We are not grocers.*
değil-siniz	**Siz bakkal değilsiniz.**	*You are not grocers.*
değil-ler	**Onlar bakkal değil(ler).**	*They are not grocers.*

Değil can be used with a noun, adjective or pronoun to make a negative sentence. For the negative of *to be*, the noun or adjective is unchanged and the personal endings are added to the word **değil**, which goes at the end of the sentence.

8 QUESTIONS WITH *TO BE*

Study the table. Notice that for a question the pronouns do not change. To review the **mı-**, **mi-**, **mu-**, **mü-** question words look back at Unit 4. When written, the two words are separate but when they are spoken they are said as one word.

Ben mi?	*Is it me?*	**Biz mi?**	*Is it us?*
Sen mi?	*Is it you?*	**Siz mi?**	*Is it you?*
O mu?	*Is it him/her/it?*	**Onlar mı?**	*Is it them?*

Now look at these questions. Notice the pronoun endings that are added to the **mi** question words.

Sekreter miyim?	*Am I a secretary?*
Öğretmen misin?	*Are you a teacher?*
Doktor mu?	*Is she/he a doctor?*
İngiliz miyiz?	*Are we English?*
İspanyol musunuz?	*Are you Spanish?*
Türk mü?/(Türk müler?)	*Are they Turks/Turkish?*

Note: The word **miyim** in **Sekreter miyim?** is made from **mi** and **im** coming together. You need a 'buffer **y**' as explained earlier. Can you spot another 'buffer **y**' in the sentences above?

9 MORE ABOUT ADJECTIVES

One of the great features of the Turkish language is that a few adjectives and nouns can get you a long way, providing you learn some word endings! Here are a few more ways of extending your word power by adding some endings.

As you saw earlier in the unit, Turkish adjectives can take personal endings.

güzel	*beautiful*
Güzeller.	*They are beautiful.*
Güzelim.	*I am beautiful.*

It is also possible to make adjectives from some nouns. For example, by adding **-lı**, **-li**, **-lu** or **-lü** to the name of many countries and cities, you change the word to an adjective or noun indicating a person from that country or city.

Kanada	*Canada*	**Kanadalı**	*from Canada*
İzmir	*Izmir*	**İzmirli**	*from Izmir*
İstanbul	*Istanbul*	**İstanbullu**	*from Istanbul*
Ürgüp	*Ürgüp*	**Ürgüplü**	*from Ürgüp*

Words indicating nationality which are formed in this way can be nouns or adjectives. So **Danimarkalı** can be translated as *Danish* (adjective) or *a Dane* (noun).

Some nationality words do not take the **-lı**, **-li**, **-lu**, **-lü** endings, for example, **Türk**, **İngiliz**, **Fransız**, **Alman**.

10 MORE WAYS OF USING THE *-LI, -Lİİ, -LU, -LÜ* ENDINGS

The endings **-lı**, **-li**, **-lu** and **-lü** are added to singular nouns to make nouns or adjectives with the following meanings:

1 **Added to the name of a quality, they mean someone or something possessing that quality:**

şeker	*sugar*	**şekerli**	*sweet*
akıl	*intelligence*	**akıllı**	*intelligent*
bulut	*cloud*	**bulutlu**	*cloudy*

2 **They can mean possessing that quality to a higher degree:**

sevgi	*affection*	**sevgili**	*beloved*
yaş	*age*	**yaşlı**	*aged, old*

3 Added to the name of a colour, they form an adjective or noun meaning dressed in that colour:

beyaz	*white*	**beyazlı**	*dressed in white*
mavi	*blue*	**mavili**	*dressed in blue*

4 These endings may be added to a phrase to extend its meaning, so:

uzun boy	*tall stature*	**uzun boylu**	*tall*
kısa saç	*short hair*	**kısa saçlı**	*short haired*
orta yaş	*middle age*	**orta yaşlı**	*middle aged*
mavi göz	*blue eyes*	**mavi gözlü**	*blue eyed*

Now that you have learned several word endings and some of the ways in which they build meaning from root words, you might start noticing that some words have combinations of these word parts:

ev	*house*
evli	*married* (lit. *with house*)
evlilik	*marriage* (lit. *the state of being with a house*)

As you saw earlier in the unit, the ending **-li** means *with* and the ending **-lik** denotes the formation of an abstract noun. You will learn more about this in Unit 9.

11 WORD ORDER AND ADJECTIVES

Now that you know how to make more adjectives, you need to make sure you put them in the correct place in the sentence. In Turkish, adjectives come before nouns, as in English:

güzel kadın	*beautiful woman*
uzun saç	*long hair*

The **bir**, which acts like the indefinite article (*a, an*), usually comes between the adjective and noun:

güzel bir kadın	*a beautiful woman* (lit. *beautiful a woman*)
yakışıklı bir erkek	*a handsome man* (lit. *handsome a man*)

12 TAG QUESTIONS

In English, tag questions vary (*wasn't it? aren't they? don't they? have you? did she?*, etc.) In Turkish, no matter what it refers to, the tag question is always **değil mi?**

Soğuk, değil mi?	*Cold, isn't it?*
Sen akıllısın, değil mi?	*You are clever, aren't you?*
Evet, akıllıyım.	*Yes, I am.*
O akıllı değil, değil mi?	*He is not clever, is he?*
Hayır, değil. (Evet, değil.)	*No, he isn't. (Yes, he is?)*

In the last example, there are two ways of expressing the same answer, but both answers show agreement that he is not clever. **Evet** or **Hayır** would be the informal short answer.

Practice

1 Match the sentences with the pictures.

a Çok güzel bir film, değil mi?
b Siz, Timur'sunuz, değil mi? Ben, Ahmet.

104

c Yiyecekler çok lezzetli, değil mi?

d Bu program çok ilginç değil, değil mi?

e Bebek çok güzel, değil mi?

f Doğru değil, değil mi?

g Burası biraz soğuk, değil mi?

h Çiçekler çok güzel, değil mi?

i Tarkan iyi bir şarkıcı, değil mi?

2 **Put the words in each sentence in the correct order. If you need help, look for the sentences in the dialogues.**

a İngilizim Ben Türk eşim ama.

b İngilizim. Hayır,

c değilim. akıllı Çok çalışkanım çok ama

d mı? yakışıklı Nişanlın

e Abla Gonca, misiniz? siz

3 **Complete the sentences with descriptive adjectives from the box. Pay attention to vowel harmony while choosing the adjectives.**

saç____	göz____	yeşil____	saç____	boy____	göz____

a Ayşe siyah _____lı.

b Banu mavi _____lü.

c Cem uzun _____lu.

d Şafak siyah _____lı ve siyah _____lü.

e _____li genç hanım Nur.

4 **Complete the sentences with the appropriate words from the box. Some may have more than one possible answer.**

yakişıklı	gramer	güzel	değil	mi	kolay
akıllı			çalışkan	işsiz	Türkçe	Türkiye

a Tarkan çok _____ bir erkek .

b Sezen Aksu çok _____ bir kadın .

c Öğretmenler çok _____ mı?

d _____ bir öğrenci.

e _____ çok ilginç.

f _____ hem tarihi hem modern bir ülke.

g Türkiye'de çok _____ var.

h Türkçe çok _____.

i İngilizce zengin bir dil, _____ _____?

j Almanca ve Fransızca _____ zor.

5 **07.10** Andy and Ayşegül are having a party at their house. The guests mingle and chat. Choose an answer from the box below to complete each conversation. Then listen to the audio to check your answers.

a Ben İstanbullu'yum.
İstanbul'un neresinden*?
_____

b Bu tatilde Türkiye'deyiz.
Türkiye'nin neresinde?
_____

c Bu Türkçe'de ne demek?
_____

d Bu İngilizce'de ne demek?
_____

e Siz manken misiniz?
Hayır, sekreterim. Ya siz?
_____

f Ben 45 yaşındayım.
_____

g Bu telefon numaram 595 33 22.
Bu da benim telefon numaram 454 78 81.
_____

h Ben İngilizim.
Gerçekten mi?
_____

i Ben bekarım. Ya, siz?
_____

j Tarkan, Alman mı?
_____

*neresinde? = *whereabouts?*

---

1 Ben evliyim. Eşim orada.
2 Evet, Londralı'yım.
3 Ben öğrenciyim.
4 Hayır, Türk.
5 Teşekkürler.
6 Harita demek.
7 Ben 23 yaşındayım.
8 Map demek.
9 Güneyde, Alanya'da.
10 Ataköy

6 Write the answers to the questions.

a Ankara nerede?

b Paris nerede?

c Londra, İngiltere'de mi?

d New York nerede?

e Moskova Rusya'da, değil mi?

Listening

07.11 **Listen to the audio, then complete the following table. The first line has been done for you.**

Name	Nationality	Job	Marital status	Age	Home town
Bülent	Turkish	doctor	—	—	İzmir
Lucy					
Trish Webb					
Philippe					
Ülkü Gezer					
June					

Speaking

07.12 **A Turkish woman engages you in conversation. Play your part in the conversation, according to the prompts.**

Listen to the conversation. Then practise role playing each part.

Turk	Merhaba.
You	*[Say 'hello']*
Turk	Ben Türküm, siz Amerikalı mısınız?
You	*[Say no, you're not American, you're English]*
Turk	Aaa! Ben bekarım. Siz evlisiniz, değil mi?
You	*[Say yes, you're married to a Turk]*
Turk	Gerçekten mi? Çok ilginç. Ben öğretmenim.
You	*[Say you're an engineer]*
Turk	Çok akıllısınız.
You	*[Return the compliment. Say she's very clever, too]*

Reading and writing

 1 **Read the text and answer the questions.**

> Ben Gurur Gizemoğlu.
> İstanbullu'yum,
> Türküm. 22 yaşındayım.
> Mühendisim.
> Siyah saçlı, siyah gözlü ve uzun
> boyluyum. Bekarım.

a Where is Gurur from?
b What is his job?
c What is he like?
d Is he married?

2 **Now write a similar text telling about yourself. Use the text above as a model.**

 ## Test yourself

 07.13 **Listen and answer the following questions orally or in writing.**

1 Ask someone if they are from America (if they are American).

2 Ask someone how old they are.

3 Ask someone what nationality they are.

4 Say you are married.

5 Ask someone if they are single.

If you get any wrong, go back through the unit and have another look before moving on to the next unit.

SELF CHECK

I CAN...

... talk about myself.

... ask other people about themselves.

... describe myself and others.

... address people correctly.

8 Alışveriş *Shopping*

In this unit you will learn how to:
▶ *shop for gifts, clothes and food.*
▶ *say what is happening.*
▶ *talk about what will happen shortly.*

CEFR: *(A1) Can handle shopping, ask for details and express preferences. Can describe what is happening now and talk about what will happen shortly.*

Shopping in Turkey

Türkiye'de alışveriş (*Shopping in Turkey*) is an experience in itself, whether you are bargaining for a **kilim** (*woven rug*) in the bustling **Kapalı Çarşı** (*Grand Bazaar*) in Istanbul, choosing **giysi** (*clothes*) in a smart **butik** (*boutique*) or buying local produce in a country **pazar** (*market*). Don't be surprised if you are offered a glass of tea as you view a range of **halı** (*carpets*) or **deri ceket** (*leather jackets*)!

Many big towns and cities have permanent covered **pazar** and **baharat pazarı** (*spice markets*). In Istanbul, the historic **Kapalı Çarşı** is an indoor maze of over 4,000 shops, selling carpets, **antika** (*antiques*), **mücevherat** (*jewellery*), **deri eşya** (*leather goods*), clothing and **tekstil** (*textiles*). Its vaulted stone passages also house banks, restaurants, **hamam** (*Turkish baths*), cafés and **cami** (*mosques*).

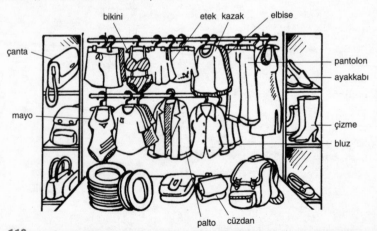

The **Mısır Çarşısı** *Egyptian Bazaar* gets its name from the ancient tradition of trade with Egypt in coffee, rice, incense and henna. Today you can still buy coffee, **baharat** (*spices*), **bitkisel çaylar** (*fruit and herbal teas*), **fıstık** (*nuts*) and **kuru yemiş** (*dried fruit*).

1 **Why would shopping in Turkey be an experience?**
2 **Where does Mısır Çarşısı get its name from? Why?**

Vocabulary builder

GÜNÜ PLANLAMA *PLANNING THE DAY*

08.01 Listen and repeat. Then complete the missing parts of the Turkish.

Bugün ne yapıyoruz?	*What are we doing today?*
Hediye _____ istiyorum.	*I want to buy gifts.*
Ben de deri ceket, ayakkabı ve lokum	*And I want to buy a leather jacket,*
_____ istiyorum.	*shoes and Turkish delight.*

NEW EXPRESSIONS

Listen to the words and phrases you will hear in the dialogues. Practise listening and saying the expressions until you feel you have learned them.

Dialogue 1 Planning the day

08.02

bugün	*today*
yapmak	*to do*
hediye	*present, gift*
almak	*to buy*
istemek	*to want*
deri	*leather*
ceket	*jacket*
ayakkabı	*shoes*
bluz	*blouse*
çanta	*bag*
baharat	*spice*
hediyelik şeyler	*suitable (things) to be used as a present*
Nereye gidelim?	*Where shall we go?*

Dialogue 2 Buying bags

08.03

çanta	*bag*
büyük	*big*
orta	*medium*
küçük	*small*
orta boy	*medium size*
sizin için	*for you*
Güle güle kullanın!*	*Enjoy using it!*

*This is a commonly used pleasantry. Its literal translation is *Use in happy days*. It's said to people who have bought or have been given something new. For clothes **Güle güle giy!** (*Enjoy wearing it!*) would be used.

Dialogue 3 Buying spices

08.04

baharat	*spice*
köftelik	*for meatballs*
kimyon	*cumin*
sumac	*sumac*
falan	*and so on/etc.*
gramlık	*gram*
paket	*packet*
başka bir şey	*anything else*
padişah macunu	*aphrodisiacs*
gerek	*necessary*
kuru yemiş	*dried fruit*
kayısı	*apricot*
yarım	*half*
incir	*fig*
fındık	*hazelnut*
fıstık	*nuts*
hepsi bu kadar	*that's all*
sudan ucuz*	*very cheap*

***Sudan ucuz** is an expression meaning *very cheap*. Literally, it means *even cheaper than water*.

Dialogue 4 Buying Turkish delight

08.05

lokumcu	*Turkish delight shop*
rica ederim	*not at all*
lokum	*Turkish delight*
çeşit	*kind, type*
naneli	*peppermint flavoured*
gül	*rose flavoured*
sade	*plain*
fıstıklı	*nutty*
yerken	*while eating*
her zaman	*always*
kiloluk	*for a kilo*
kutu	*box*
1777'den beri	*since 1777*
taze	*fresh*
her	*every*
tüm	*all*
dünya	*world*
satmak	*to sell*
değişik	*different*
koymak	*to put*
tariff	*recipe*
sırrımız	*our secret*
özel	*special*
ziyaret	*visit*
birbirimiz	*each other*
hep	*all*
olarak	*as*
vermek	*to give*

Dialogue 5 Buying clothes

08.06

bluz	*blouse*
bakmak	*to look*
Kaç beden?	*What size?*
yakışmak	*to suit*
denemek	*to try on*
pazarlık	*bargaining*
pazarlık yapmak	*to bargain, haggle*
sizin için	*for you*

Look at the items in the suitcase. Practise reading them and saying them out loud until you feel you have learned them.

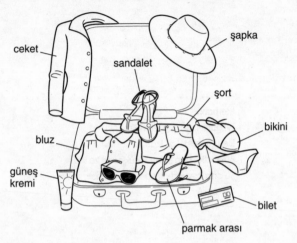

Dialogues

Read the introduction and the gist question for each conversation. Then listen or read the conversation and answer the questions.

1 PLANNING THE DAY

 08.07 *Laura and Ben are talking about what they are going to do.*

1 What do they want to do today?

Ben	Bugün ne yapıyoruz?
Laura	Bilmiyorum. Ben hediye almak istiyorum*.
Ben	Ben de deri ceket, ayakkabı ve lokum almak istiyorum.
Laura	Kapalı Çarşı'ya gidelim mi? *(Laura looks at her shopping list.)*
	Bluz, çanta, baharat, ayakkabı ve hediyelik şeyler.
Ben	Nereye gidelim?
Laura	Ben Kapalı Çarşı'ya ve Taksim'e gitmek istiyorum.
Ben	Tamam, gidelim.

*The verb **istemek** means *to want*; **istiyorum** means *I want* (lit. *I am wanting*).

2 What does Ben want to do?

3 Where are they going to go?

2 BUYING BAGS

 08.08 Later on, in Istanbul's Grand Bazaar Laura is talking to the **satıcı** *(salesperson).*

1 What does Laura want to buy?

Laura	Merhaba.
Satıcı	İyi günler. Buyrun, efendim.
Laura	Deri çantalar kaç lira?
Satıcı	Büyük 80, orta 50 ve küçükler de 20 lira.
Laura	Şu orta boy, lütfen. 50 lira çok pahalı, 30 lira olur mu?
Satıcı	Ne renk?
Laura	Siyah, lütfen.
Satıcı	Buyrun. Sizin için 40 lira.
Laura	Tamam. *(Laura hands over the money.)*
Satıcı	Güle güle kullanın.
Laura	Teşekkür ederim.

* **Buyrun** means *Go ahead, feel free* or *What can I do for you?*, but it can also mean *Here you are.*

2 Does Laura haggle?

3 BUYING SPICES

 08.09 Laura and Ben walk to the spice market to buy spices and dried fruit. They talk to the **tezgahtar** *(stall owner).*

1 What kinds of spice does Laura want to buy?

Tezgahtar	Buyrun?
Laura	Baharat almak istiyoruz.
Tezgahtar	Neler almak istiyorsunuz?
Laura	Köftelik baharat, kimyon, sumak falan.
Tezgahtar	Ne kadar?
Laura	Yüz gramlık paketler.
Tezgahtar	Başka bir şey istiyor musunuz?

Ben	Bu ne?
Tezgahtar	Padişah macunu.
Ben	Padişah macunu ne demek?
Tezgahtar	Afrodizyak demek.
Ben	Benim için gerek yok. Ben istemiyorum. (laughter) Biraz kuru yemiş istiyorum.
Tezgahtar	Ne kadar?
Ben	Yarım kilo kayısı, yarım kilo incir. Fındık var mı? Güzel mi?
(The stall owner offers them some nuts to try.)	
Ben	Evet! Yarım kilo karışık fıstık, lütfen. Hepsi bu kadar. Kaç lira?
Tezgahtar	10 lira. Sudan ucuz!

2 Does Ben want any aphrodisiac?

3 What quantity of mixed nuts does Ben want to buy?

4 BUYING TURKISH DELIGHT

 08.10 *Having bought their spices, Laura and Ben want to buy Turkish delight from the famous Hacı Bekir Turkish delight and sweet shop. Laura is asking a* **yaya** *(passer by) for directions.*

1 Do Laura and Ben haggle?

Laura	Afedersiniz, Hacı Bekir Lokumcusu nerede?
Yaya	Düz gidin, sağa dönün, solda.
Laura	Teşekkürler.
Yaya	Rica ederim.
(They go into the Hacı Bekir sweet shop.)	
Tezgahtar	Buyrun, efendim.
Laura	Lokum almak istiyoruz, kaç lira?
Tezgahtar	Hangi çeşit?
Ben	Neler var?
(The assistant holds out a tray of free samples, pointing out the different types.)	
Tezgahtar	Bu naneli, bu gül, bu sade, bu da fıstıklı. Buyrun. Tatlı yiyelim, tatlı konuşalım.* Tatlı yerken biz her zaman böyle diyoruz.
Laura and Ben	Mmmm.
(Laura and Ben both love the Turkish delight, and they decide to buy some of their gifts from here.)	

Tezgahtar	Yarım kilo karışık 10 lira.
Laura	Yarım kiloluk dört kutu karışık, lütfen.

(While their Turkish delight is being put into special boxes, wrapped and sealed, Ben asks some questions.)

Ben	Dükkan yeni mi?
Tezgahtar	Hayır, biz 1777'den beri lokum yapıyoruz. Lokumlarımız çok taze. Her gün yeni lokum geliyor. Bugün tüm dünyaya satıyoruz. Her hafta değişik bir çeşit yapıyoruz.
Ben	Nasıl yapıyorsunuz?
Tezgahtar	Şeker, fıstık ve ... koyuyoruz ama tarifi bizim sırrımız.
Ben	Lokumu daha çok turistlere mi satıyorsunuz?
Tezgahtar	Hayır, biz Türkler özel günlerde ve ziyaretlerde birbirimize hep hediye olarak lokum veriyoruz.

Tatlı yiyelim tatlı konuşalım Let's eat sweet, speak sweet is a common saying when offering sweets.

2 Do they get the recipe for Turkish delight?

3 How many boxes of Turkish delight do they buy?

> **TIP**
>
> **Lokum** comes in various flavours: **gülsuyu** (*rosewater*), **meyve** (*fruit*) or **nane** (*peppermint*), and it is sometimes filled with **çamfısığı** (*pistachios*), **fındık** (*hazelnuts*) or **kayısı** (*apricots*). **Lokum** remains popular among Turks and tourists alike. It tends to be eaten on special occasions, holidays, birthdays and with coffee. It also makes an ideal gift if you are invited to someone's house.

5 BUYING CLOTHES

 08.11 *Later that afternoon, Laura goes to a clothing shop. She is talking to the* **satış elemanı** *(shop assistant).*

1 What does Laura want to buy?

Satış elemanı	Buyrun, efendim.
Laura	Bir bluz bakıyorum.
Satış elemanı	Kaç beden?*
Laura	38.
Satış elemanı	Buyrun. Bu bluz çok güzel.
Laura	Yeşil bana yakışmıyor. Mavi veya beyaz var mı?
Satış elemanı	Buyrun. Bir mavi, bir beyaz, 38 beden.
Laura	Kaç lira?

Satış elemanı	70 lira.
Laura	Denemek istiyorum.
Satış elemanı	Tabii.
(Laura tries it on.)	
Laura	Bunu alıyorum. Kaç lira?
Satış elemanı	70 lira.
Laura	Çok pahalı. 50 lira veriyorum.
Satış elemanı	Burada pazarlık yapmıyoruz. Sizin için 60 lira.
Laura	Tamam, alıyorum.

*Turkish sizes for clothing and shoes are the same as European sizes.

2 **What does Laura buy?**

3 **Does she haggle?**

Language discovery

1 **Answer these questions about the dialogues. Use Turkish where possible.**
   a How does Ben say *what are we doing today*?
   b How does Ben say *I don't want it*?
   c How does Laura say *I'm looking for a blouse*?
   d How does Laura say *I'd like to try it on*?

2 **Notice what the sentences below have in common. What comes after the main part of the verbs? The answer is in the box.**
   a Hediye almak istiyorum.
   b Her gün lokum geliyor.
   c Tüm dünyaya satıyoruz.
   d Şeker, fıstık ... koyuyoruz.
   e Yüzüyoruz.

> The verbs all include some form of **-yor**; this is the **-iyor** present tense.
>
> The verbs all come at the end of the sentences.
>
> For the explanation of the **-iyor** tense, see Section 1 in Go further.

3 **Find more examples of this tense in the dialogues and highlight them.**

4 **Practise the dialogues, using your name and the names of people you know.**

8 Alışveriş Shopping

Go further

1 THE -IYOR PRESENT TENSE: WHAT'S HAPPENING

In the dialogues, you will notice a new tense, the **-iyor** present tense. You use this tense to say what is happening right now. However, it has different usages. For example, in Dialogue 5, Laura says, **Bunu alıyorum** (*I'll take it*). This literally means *I'm taking it*.

The **-iyor** tense has several purposes. These are shown in the following table.

Purpose	Example	Translation
Describing something happening now	**Alışveriş yapıyoruz.**	*We're shopping.*
Stating an unchanging fact	**Alkol kullanmıyorum.**	*I don't drink alcohol.*
Describing a habitual repeated action	**Türkler sık sık çay içiyorlar.**	*Turks often drink tea.*
Describing something that will happen soon	**Bugün alışveriş yapıyoruz.**	*We're shopping today.*
Stating how long you have been doing something	**1777'den beri lokum yapıyoruz/satıyoruz.**	*We've been making/ selling Turkish delight since 1777.*

The **-iyor** present tense is also used to express senses and emotions which in English are expressed in the simple present tense: **Biliyorum.** *I know.* (lit. *I'm knowing.*), **Seviyorum.** *I love.* (lit. *I'm loving.*), **Görüyorum.** *I see/I can see.* (lit. *I'm seeing.*), **İşitiyorum.** *I hear/I can hear.* (lit. *I'm hearing.*), **Hissediyorum.** *I feel.* (lit. *I'm feeling.*).

To use this tense, you need to remember to add two verb endings: the tense ending and the correct ending for the equivalent of the verb *to be*.

For the **-iyor** present tense, the endings are as follows:

1 For the tense:

Add **-ıyor, -iyor, -uyor, -üyor** (according to the rules of vowel harmony), or simply **-yor** after a verb ending in a vowel. If the verb stem ends in **a** or **e**, these vowels are replaced by **ı** and **i** respectively.

2 For the equivalent of the verb *to be* ending:

-um	*I*	**-uz**	*we*
-sun	*you*	**-sunuz**	*you*
(none)	*he/she/it*	**-ler/lar**	*they*

For example, *to buy/take/get/receive* is **almak**.

Stem	Tense ending *-ing*	Verb *to be* ending	
al-	-ıyor	-um	**Alıyorum.** *I am buying.*

Thus, you might literally translate **alıyorum** as follows:

al	**-ıyor**	**-um**
take	*-ing*	*I am*

The verb *want/would like* is **istemek**; the stem is **iste-** but the **e** changes to **i**:

Stem	Tense ending *-ing*	Verb *to be* ending	
iste-	-iyor	-um	**Istiyorum.** *I want/would like*

Study these sample verbs:

	istemek *to want/ would like*	**ödemek** *to pay*	**almak** *to buy/take/ get/receive*
I	istiyorum	ödüyorum	alıyorum
you	istiyorsun	ödüyorsun	alıyorsun
he/she/it	istiyor	ödüyor	alıyor
we	istiyoruz	ödüyoruz	alıyoruz
you	istiyorsunuz	ödüyorsunuz	alıyorsunuz
they	istiyorlar	ödüyorlar	alıyorlar

2 NEGATIVES: WHAT'S NOT HAPPENING

Notice the **m** after the verb stems in these examples.

Onu almıyorum.	*I am not buying that.*
Şapka giymiyorum.	*I am not wearing a hat.*
Yüzmüyor.	*He/She is not swimming.*
Okumuyorsun.	*You are not reading.*

If you want to make a verb negative in the **-iyor** present tense, you add **-m** to the stem before the **-iyor/-yor** ending.

3 QUESTIONS: WHAT'S HAPPENING?

Notice the **mu-** question ending before the equivalent of the verb *to be* ending.

Alıyor musun?	*Are you buying?*
Deri seviyor musunuz?	*Do you like leather?*
Kredi kartı alıyor musunuz?	*Do you take credit cards?*

In the written form, the two parts of the verb are separate, though they are spoken as one word:

Note: When you make questions using question words such as **Ne?** (*What?*), **Kaç?** (*How much/many?*), **Kim?** (*Who?*), **Nasıl?** (*How is it?/What is it like?*), **Nerede?** (*Where?*), **Neden?** (*Why?*), **Niçin?** (*Why?*), etc. you don't use **mu-** or its variations – you use the question word instead:

Ne istiyorsunuz?	*What would you like?*
Kaç tane istiyorsunuz?	*How many do you want?*

4 WORDS SIMILAR TO ENGLISH

Words that are cognates with English are easy to remember. Here are some words related to this unit's theme: **plan** (*plan*), **ceket** (*jacket*), **bluz** (*blouse*), **sumak** (*sumac*), **gram** (*gram*), **paket** (*packet*), **kilo** (*kilo*), **turist** (*tourist*), **şort** (*shorts*), **sterlin** (*sterling*). Practise saying them out loud in Turkish.

5 PAIRS

In English, some items of clothing are usually spoken of as being in a pair, such as a pair of shoes, socks, gloves or slippers. You can choose to translate this expression literally in Turkish: **Bir çift ayakkabı almak istiyorum** (*I'd like to buy a pair of shoes*). If you say **Ayakkabı almak istiyorum** (*I'd like to buy shoes*), your listener will normally assume that you want a pair of shoes.

However, English also talks of pairs of trousers, glasses and tights, while actually referring to only one item. You would always refer to **bir pantolon** (*trousers*), **külotlu çorap** (*tights*), **gözlük** (*glasses*). If you asked for **pantolonlar** in Turkey, the shopkeeper would think you wanted more than one pair!

bir pantolon	*a pair of trousers*
bir çift ayakkabı	*a pair of shoes*
bir gözlük	*a pair of glasses*
şort	*(a pair of) shorts*
Pantolon almak istiyorum.	*I'd like to buy a pair of trousers.*
(Bir çift) ayakkabı almak istiyorum.	*I'd like to buy a pair of shoes.*

6 *GİYMEK* OR *TAKMAK*

The verb **giymek** is used when we talk about wearing clothes, but **takmak** is used for jewellery and accessories.

Siyah, deri ceket giyiyor.	*He/she is wearing a black leather jacket.*
Saat takıyor ama yüzük takmıyor.	*He/she is wearing a watch but not a ring.*

Practice

1 **Match the Turkish words with their English equivalents.**

a	ceket		1	sterling
b	bluz		2	shorts
c	turist		3	jacket
d	şort		4	tourist
e	sterlin		5	blouse

2 08.12 A woman is in a clothing shop talking to the salesperson. Unscramble the following dialogue. Then listen to the audio to check your answers or look in the Answer key.

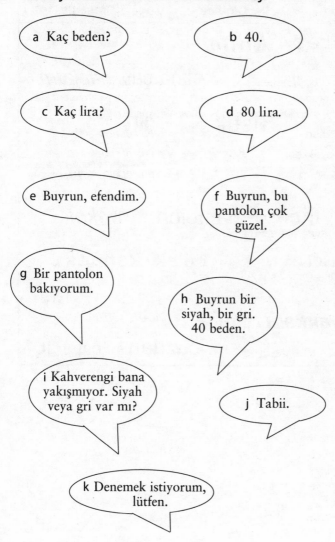

a Kaç beden?

b 40.

c Kaç lira?

d 80 lira.

e Buyrun, efendim.

f Buyrun, bu pantolon çok güzel.

g Bir pantolon bakıyorum.

h Buyrun bir siyah, bir gri. 40 beden.

i Kahverengi bana yakışmıyor. Siyah veya gri var mı?

j Tabii.

k Denemek istiyorum, lütfen.

3 Here are some items that you might like to buy in Turkey. Sort them into groups under the headings supplied:

Food	Clothes	Presents

çerez   kilim

elma çay   *lokum*

fıstık   **T-shirt**

padişah macunu   **CD**   *bluz*

incir   pantolon   *ceket*

kaset   çanta   Türk kahvesi

halı

ayakkabı   *bal*

cüzdan   baharat

elma çay	*apple tea*
kaset	*tape*
halı	*carpet*
cüzdan	*wallet, purse*

4 Put the verb stems in the box in positive and negative -ing forms. The first one is done for you. Just use the *-iyor* tense ending (ignore the personal endings). As a challenge, find these verbs in the dialogues.

yap	iste	gel	koy	oku	yüz	yakış	dene

	positive		negative
a	yapıyor		yapmıyor
b	_____		_____
c	_____		_____
d	_____		_____
e	_____		_____
f	_____		_____
g	_____		_____
h	_____		_____

5 Look at the suitcase for three minutes. Then write down as many items as you can remember in Turkish.

6 Draw your ideal *gardırop* wardrobe and label the items.

Speaking

 08.13 **Listen to the conversation. You are buying a leather jacket. Then practise role playing each part.**

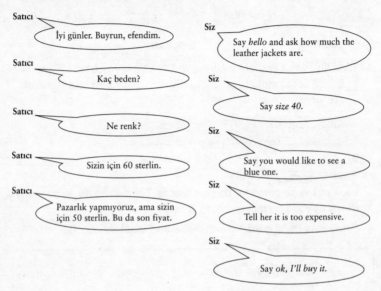

Satıcı: İyi günler. Buyrun, efendim.

Siz: Say *hello* and ask how much the leather jackets are.

Satıcı: Kaç beden?

Siz: Say *size 40*.

Satıcı: Ne renk?

Siz: Say you would like to see a blue one.

Satıcı: Sizin için 60 sterlin.

Satıcı: Pazarlık yapmıyoruz, ama sizin için 50 sterlin. Bu da son fiyat.

Siz: Tell her it is too expensive.

Siz: Say *ok, I'll buy it*.

 Reading and writing

  1 08.14 **Picture dictation. Read or listen to the Turkish passage that follows. Draw the scene on a piece of paper and then check it with the answer in the Answer key at the back of the book.**

Suzan deniz kenarında bir kafede oturuyor. Meyve suyu içerken plajda ve denizdeki insanlara bakıyor. Üç çocuk dondurma alıyor. Bir çift kumlarda yatıyor. Bikinili ve şapkalı kadın kitap okuyor. Şortlu ve gözlüklü erkek denize bakıyor. Denizde bir sandal ve bir yelkenli var. Yedi kişi yüzüyor.

oturuyor	*sitting (**oturmak** to sit)*
plaj	*beach*
insanlar	*people*
çift	*couple*
yatıyor	*lying (**yatmak** to lie down)*
okuyor	*reading (**okumak** to read)*

kitap	book
şort	shorts
sandal	rowing boat
yelkenli	sailing boat
kişi	person
yüzüyor	swimming (**yüzmek** to swim)

2 **Describe what you are wearing today. Use giymek (***to wear clothing***) or takmak (***to wear jewellery or accessories***) and some of these words.**

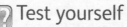

şapka   gözlük   bluz   T-shirt   pantolon
şort   ceket   ayakkabı   saat   yüzük

saat = *watch*

yüzük = *ring*

Test yourself

08.15 Listen and answer the following questions orally or in writing.

1 Ask for a blue jacket in size 40.
2 Ask for some peppermint-flavoured Turkish delight.
3 Ask for half a kilo of dried fruit.
4 Buy a packet of cumin.
5 Say *I don't drink wine* in Turkish.

SELF CHECK

	I CAN...
◯	...shop for gifts, clothes and food.
◯	...say what is happening.
◯	...talk about what will happen shortly.

9 Nereye gidelim?
Where shall we go?

In this unit you will learn how to:
▶ *make arrangements to go out or suggest doing something.*
▶ *tell the time.*
▶ *make reservations for a performance.*
▶ *buy tickets for public transport.*
▶ *make, accept or refuse an invitation.*

CEFR *(A2): Can describe plans and arrangements. Can ask and tell the time, buy tickets and invite people to events and respond to invitations.*

 Cinema and theatre

Sinema (*cinema*) and **tiyatro** (*theatre*) are a very popular form of **eğlence** (*entertainment*) in Turkey. There are several **film festivalleri** (*film festivals*) in Turkey. Most foreign films are shown in the **orijinal** (*original*) language, with Turkish subtitles. The Istanbul International Film Festival in the spring shows some Turkish films with foreign subtitles.

If you have the opportunity, it is worth watching a Turkish film as it will give you a greater insight into Turkish **kültür** (*culture*). A good example is the Turkish film ***Hamam*** (*The Turkish Bath*), which tells the story of an Italian who inherited a Turkish bath and leaves Italy to go to Turkey to run it. Subtitled films provide an opportunity for you to hear Turkish being spoken and maybe even understand some of it.

The **Kenterler** are a brother and sister who established the first successful **özel tiyatro** (*private theatre company*); it is still famous for high-quality **prodüksiyon** (*productions*).

The theatre is just a 10-minute walk from **Taksim Meydanı** (*Taksim Square*) and would be an invaluable experience. The types of productions are usually classics, and you can expect to see a variety of traditional Turkish and international plays. For more information go to www://Kentertiyatrosu.org/.

Vocabulary builder

HAFTA SONU *THE WEEKEND*

09.01 Listen and repeat. Then complete the missing parts of the Turkish expressions.

A: Hafta sonunda ne yapalım?	*What shall we do at the weekend?*
B: Tiyatroya gidelim mi? Kenterler'de çok güzel bir oyun var.	*Shall we go to the theatre? There's a very good play on at the Kenterler.*
A: Ne o _____?	*What's on?*
B: Bakalım. Galiba Hep Aşk Vardı o _____.	*Let's have a look. I think There Has Always Been Love is on.*

ZAMAN *TIME*

09.02 Listen and repeat. Draw a clock face and put your notes on it.

saat	*time/hour/clock*
Saat kaç?	*What time is it?*
Saat kaçta?	*At what time?*
Kaç saat?	*How many hours?*
dakika	*minutes*
saniye	*seconds*
çeyrek	*a quarter*
buçuk	*it's half past*
buçukta	*at half past*
geçiyor (-ı, -i, -u, -ü)	*past*
var (-e, -a)	*to*
öğlen	*midday*
gece yarısı	*midnight*

NEW EXPRESSIONS

Listen to the words and phrases you will hear in the dialogues. Practise listening and saying the expressions until you feel you have learned them.

Dialogue 1 Weekend plans

09.03

hafta	*week*
hafta sonu	*weekend*
Ne yapalım?	*What shall we do?*
tiyatro	*theatre*
Gidelim mi?	*Shall we go?*
Ne oynuyor?	*What's on?*
bakalım	*let's have a look*
galiba	*I think/perhaps, maybe*
da	*also*
görmek	*to see*
istiyorum	*I want/I would like*
aramak	*to call*
arayayım	*let me call (I'll call)*
hadi, arayalım	*let's call*
yarım	*half past twelve*
bir buçukta	*at half past one*
tamam	*OK*

Dialogue 2 Theatre reservations

09.04

buyrun	*Yes, I'm listening to you! How can I help you? (said on the phone)*
bilet	*ticket*
ayırtmak	*to book, to reserve*
maalesef	*unfortunately*
gelecek	*next, coming*
yer	*place, seat*
fiyatlar	*prices*
nasıl	*how*
tam	*adult/full price*
öğrenci	*student*
emekli	*retired*
ödemek	*to pay*
kartla	*by card*
kart/kredi kartı	*card/credit card*

Dialogue 3 Choosing a film

09.05

akşam	*evening*
hadi	*let's*
korku	*horror*

komedi	*comedy*
dolmuşla	*by **dolmuş** (shared taxi)*
otobüsle	*by bus*
bozuk	*broken, not working*
rahat	*comfortable*
neyle	*by what* (lit. *how*)

Dialogue 4 Buying bus tickets

09.06

dönüş	*return (trip)*
bozuk	*change*
otobüs	*bus/coach*
uçak	*aeroplane*
vapur	*ferry*
dolmuş	*shared taxi*
taksi	*taxi*
metro	*underground*
metrobüs	*tube bus*
bisiklet	*bicycle*
araba	*car*
otobüs durağı	*bus stop*
istasyon	*station*
havaalanı	*airport*
iskele	*port*
dolmuş durağı	***dolmuş** stop*
taksi durağı	*taxi rank*
istasyon	*station*
durak	*stop*

> **TIP**
>
> In some towns shared taxis called **dolmuş** operate on certain routes. **Dolmuş** only go when they are full (**dolmuş** literally means *it is filled up*). You can get on and off the **dolmuş** at any point along its route. **Dolmuş** are cheaper than ordinary taxis. The price is in proportion to the distance you travel. You can recognise a **dolmuş** by the sign on the roof or windscreen.

LEISURE ACTIVITIES

09.07 Here is a list of leisure activities.

alışveriş yapmak	*to go shopping*
sinemaya gitmek	*to go to the cinema*
tiyatroya gitmek	*to go to the theatre*
restorana gitmek	*to go to a restaurant*
müzeye gitmek	*to go to the museum*
televizyon seyretmek	*to watch TV*

müzik dinlemek	*to listen to music*
yüzmek	*to swim*
seyahat etmek	*to travel*

Dialogues

Read the introduction and the gist question for each dialogue. Then listen or read the conversation and answer the questions.

1 WEEKEND PLANS

 09.08 *Banu and Şafak are talking about what to do this weekend.*

1 What type of entertainment are Şafak and Banu discussing?

Şafak	Hafta sonunda ne yapalım?
Banu	Tiyatroya gidelim mi? Kenterler'de çok güzel bir oyun var.
Şafak	Ne oynuyor?
Banu	Bakalım. Galiba Hep Aşk Vardı oynuyor.
(They look at the Kenter Theatre's schedule.)	
Şafak	Hep Aşk Vardı oynuyor, saat 8.30'da.
Banu	Evet, harika. Ben Hamam'ı da görmek istiyorum ama.
Şafak	Hamam'ı ben de görmek istiyorum.
Banu	Önce Kenterler'i arayayım mı?
Şafak	Hadi, arayalım.
(The telephone rings, but there is no reply.)	
Şafak	Saat kaç?
Banu	Yarım. Öğle tatili.
Şafak	Bir buçukta tekrar arayalım.
Banu	Tamam.

2 What do they decide to do?

2 THEATRE RESERVATIONS

 09.09 *Şafak is calling the theatre about tickets.*

1 What is Şafak asking about?

Resepsiyon memuru[1]	Buyrun. 0212 246 35 89, Kenter Tiyatrosu.
Şafak	İyi günler. Bu pazar Hep Aşk Vardı için iki bilet ayırtmak istiyoruz.
Resepsiyon memuru	İyi günler, efendim. Maalesef bu pazar için hiç bilet yok ama gelecek pazar için yer var.

Şafak	Fiyatlar nasıl acaba?
Resepsiyon memuru	Tam 30 Lira, öğrenci 15 Lira, öğretmen ve emekli 20 Lira.
Şafak	İki bilet, bir tam ve bir öğrenci, lütfen.
Resepsiyon memuru	Nasıl ödüyorsunuz? Kartla[2] mı?
Şafak	Evet.
Resepsiyon memuru	Kart numaranız, lütfen?
Şafak	1234 1234 1234 1234.

[1] **Resepsiyon memuru** = *receptionist*

[2] **Kartla** = *with a card/by card*

2   How many tickets do they want to reserve?

3   How does Şafak pay?

3 CHOOSING A FILM

09.10 *Banu and Şafak are discussing which film to see.*

1   Which film do they decide to see?

Şafak	Bu akşam sinemaya gidiyor muyuz?
Banu	Hadi Hamam'ı[1] görelim.
Şafak	Bakalım sinemalarda hangi filmler var.
Banu	ABC'de Vampirler[2] var.
Şafak	Ben korku filmi görmek istemiyorum.
Banu	Hisar'da Şaban[3] oynuyor.
Şafak	O komedi değil mi?
Banu	Evet, ama ben Hamam'ı görmek istiyorum.
Şafak	Saat kaçta?
(Banu looks at the newspaper.)	
Banu	Beşte, yedide ve dokuzda.
Şafak	Yediye gidelim mi?
Banu	Tamam. Hadi şimdi çıkalım.
Şafak	Araba bozuk. Dolmuşla mı, otobüsle mi gidiyoruz? Otobüs daha ucuz, dolmuş daha rahat.
Banu	Fark etmez.
Şafak	Hadi otobüsle gidelim.

[1] **Hamam** = *Turkish bath*

[2] **Vampirler** = *vampires*

[3] **Şaban** = *stupid*

2 How are they getting to the cinema?

4 BUYING BUS TICKETS

 09.11 *Şafak and Banu go to the nearest bus stop to buy tickets for the bus.*

> **TIP**
> In Istanbul, you need to buy your bus ticket before you get on a bus.

1 Do they buy single or return tickets?

Şafak	Taksim'e iki bilet.
Banu	Dönüş için de al.
(At the ticket office.)	
Şafak	Dört bilet, lütfen.
Memur	Dört lira.
(Şafak hands over a 10 lira note.)	
Şafak	Buyrun.
Memur	Bozuk yok mu?
Şafak	Yok.
Memur	*(handing over the change)* Buyrun. Altı lira.

2 How much are the tickets?

 Language discovery

1 **Answer these questions about the dialogues. Use Turkish where possible.**

   a How does Şafak ask *What shall we do at the weekend*?
   b How does Şafak ask *What time is it*?
   c How does Banu agree that they should leave now?
   d How does Şafak suggest that they should take a bus?

2 **Practise the dialogues, using your name and the names of people you know.**

3 **Match the questions and answers.**

   a Önce Kenterler'i arayayım mı?   1 Otobüsle.
   b Saat kaç?   2 Hadi şimdi çıkalım.
   c Nasıl ödüyorsunuz?   3 Kartla mı? Fark etmez.
   d Yediye gidelim mi?   4 Yok.
   e Dolmuşla mı, otobüsle mi gidiyoruz?   5 Hadi arayalım.
   f Bozuk yok mu?   6 Öğle tatili.

4 *Saat kaç?* or *Kaç saat?* **While both these questions relate to time, they have different meanings:**

Saat kaç?   *What time is it?*

Kaç saat?   *How many hours? How long?*

>
> Turkish word order is generally flexible; however in some cases, rearranging the word order can create a difference in meaning.

5 **Find these sentences in Dialogue 1. Which connecting letter is inserted between the two vowels? Notice how much easier it is to say with the connecting consonant. What do we call this letter?**
   a Tiyatro_a gidelim mi?
   b Hadi ara_alım.

6 **Find this sentence in Dialogue 3. Fill in the two blanks.**

Dolmuş_____ mı, otobüs_____ mi gidiyoruz?

The ending **-ile** means *by/by means of transport*. A shortened version is used above according to vowel harmony.

Go further

1 MAKING SUGGESTIONS, OFFERING HELP, ACCEPTING OR REFUSING AN OFFER

The endings discussed here cover a variety of situations, including making a suggestion, offering or refusing help and making a suggestion about what to do or not to do. Not all the examples have an exact translation in English, but most are somewhat similar to *let*.

1 The *let* meaning of verbs

Look at the following examples, meaning *let*:

Yapayım	(me)	*Let me do/make..., I'll do/make..., I'd better do it.*
Yapalım	(us)	*Let's do/make..., We'd better do it.*
Yapsın	(his/her)	*Let him/her do/make..., He/She should do/make..., He'd/She'd better do it.*
Yapsınlar	(them)	*Let them do/make..., They should do/make..., They'd better do it.*

2 Making suggestions, offering help with -eyim or -ayım

yardım et

Yardım edeyim.	*Let me help./I'll help.*

ara

Tiyatroyu arayayım.	*Let me call the theatre./I'll call the theatre.*

3 Making suggestions, offering help with -eyim mi? or -ayım mı?

Yardım edeyim mi?	*Shall I help?*
Sinemayı arayayım mı?	*Shall I call the cinema?*

4 Accepting or refusing an offer with -meyeyim, -mayayım

Şimdi aramayayım.	*I don't want to call now. (lit. Let me not call now.)*
Tiyatroya gitmeyeyim.	*I don't want to go to the theatre. (lit. Let me not go to the theatre.)*

5 Suggesting doing something together with -elim, -alım

Gidelim.	*Let's go.*
Bakalım.	*Let's have a look./Go on then.*

6 Suggesting doing something with -elim mi? or -alım mı?

Gidelim mi?	*Shall we go?*
Bakalım mı?	*Let's have a look, shall we?*

7 Suggesting what not to do with -meyelim or -mayalım

Gitmeyelim.	*Let's not go.*
Bakmayalım.	*Let's not look.*

2 TELLING THE TIME

There are two ways of telling the time in Turkish: the 24-hour clock and the 12-hour clock. The 24-hour clock is used at airports and stations and also on the radio and television. However, for everyday purposes Turkish people use the 12-hour clock.

When you are talking about time in Turkish, there is no distinction between a.m. and p.m. Usually, people will be able to tell if you are talking about morning, afternoon or evening by the context of the conversation. But just to make sure, you can add the Turkish for the period of the day and say **sabah sekizde** (*at eight in the morning*), **öğleden sonra üçte** (*at three in the afternoon*), **akşam altıda** (*at six in the evening*), **gece onda** (*at ten at night*).

3 SAAT KAÇ? *WHAT TIME IS IT?*

09.12

The 24-hour clock

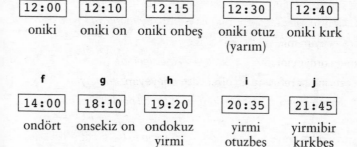

a	b	c	d	e
12:00	12:10	12:15	12:30	12:40
oniki	oniki on	oniki onbeş	oniki otuz (yarım)	oniki kırk

f	g	h	i	j
14:00	18:10	19:20	20:35	21:45
ondört	onsekiz on	ondokuz yirmi	yirmi otuzbeş	yirmibir kırkbeş

The 12-hour clock

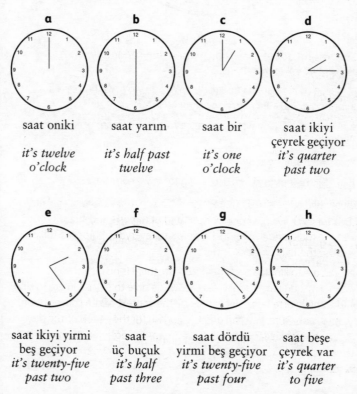

a saat oniki
it's twelve o'clock

b saat yarım
it's half past twelve

c saat bir
it's one o'clock

d saat ikiyi çeyrek geçiyor
it's quarter past two

e saat ikiyi yirmi beş geçiyor
it's twenty-five past two

f saat üç buçuk
it's half past three

g saat dördü yirmi beş geçiyor
it's twenty-five past four

h saat beşe çeyrek var
it's quarter to five

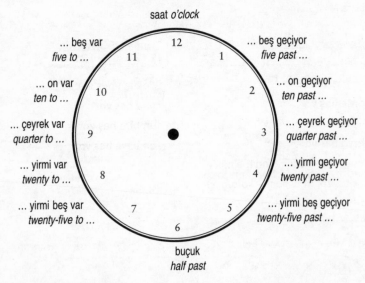

The effect of vowel harmony

Look at clock **d** in the previous section. Why do we say **ikiyi çeyrek geçiyor** and not just **iki çeyrek geçiyor**?

Look at clock **h**. Why do we say **beşe çeyrek var** and not simply **beş çeyrek var**?

1 Past the hour – geçiyor

-ı (**-i**, **-u**, **-ü**) endings are used according to vowel harmony:

Formula: hour + minutes past + **geçiyor**

biri beş geçiyor *five past one*	**yediyi beş geçiyor**
ikiyi beş geçiyor	**sekizi beş geçiyor**
üçü beş geçiyor	**dokuzu beş geçiyor**
dördü beş geçiyor	**onu beş geçiyor**
beşi beş geçiyor	**on biri beş geçiyor**
altıyı beş geçiyor	**on ikiyi beş geçiyor**

Notice the **-ı** ending (the direct object) on the hour.

2 To the hour – var

When **var** is used, the hour must adopt the ending **-e** or **-a** according to vowel harmony:

Formula : hour + **-e** or **-a** ending + minutes to + **var**

bire beş var *five to one*	**yediye beş var**
ikiye beş var	**sekize beş var**
üçe beş var	**dokuza beş var**
dörde beş var	**ona beş var**
beşe beş var	**on bire beş var**
altıya beş var	**on ikiye beş var**

Notice the **-e** ending on the hour.

3 at ... to, at ... past – kala/geçe

saat sekize beş kala	*at five to eight*
saat sekizi beş geçe	*at five past one*

Here, you use the word **kala** instead of **var**, and **geçe** instead of **geçiyor**.

5 THE 'BUFFER Y'

Notice if there are two vowels next to each other you insert a connecting **y** to make it easier to say, e.g., **bakmayalım**, **yardım edeyim**. (For a fuller explanation see Unit 5.)

6 CONSONANT CHANGE

In addition to the 'buffer **y**' there are also some consonant changes in Turkish. The hard consonants are: **ç, f, h, k, p, s, ş** and **t**. Try pronouncing each one.

When a hard consonant is followed by an ending which usually starts with a **d**, you must change the **d** to a **t**. This is similar to vowel harmony, but with consonants. At this stage do not worry about getting all these changes right. It is enough for you to recognise them.

Saat kaçda? becomes **saat kaçta?**	*At what time?*
Saat üçde becomes **saat üçte**.	*At three o'clock.*
Saat dörtde becomes **saat dörtte**.	*At four o'clock.*

7 İLE BY/BY MEANS OF

The word **ile** means *by/by means of* when referring to transport. When **ile** is shortened to an ending in spoken Turkish, it becomes **-le** or **-la** and follows the rules for vowel harmony, in the same way as the **-ler** and **-lar** endings explained in Unit 2.

Neyle (ne + ile) gidiyorsun?	*How are you getting there?* (lit. *What are you going with/by?*)
Otobüs ile gidiyorum. } **Otobüsle gidiyorum.** }	*I'm going by* (lit. *with*) *bus.*
Vapur ile gidiyorum. } **Vapurla gidiyorum.** }	*I'm going by boat.*

8 WORDS SIMILAR TO ENGLISH

Here are some cognates related to this unit's theme: **kart** (*card*), **sinema** (*cinema*), **film** (*film*), **komedi** (*comedy*), **dokümanter** (*documentary*), **taksi** (*taxi*), **tren** (*train*), **metrobüs** (*tube bus*), **istasyon** (*station*), **TV/ televizyon** (*television*), **program** (*programme*), **müzik** (*music*). Practise saying them out loud in Turkish.

Practice

1 09.14 **Here is a list of leisure activities. First check their meanings in the vocabulary list.**

alışveriş yapmak _____
sinemaya gitmek _____
tiyatroya gitmek _____
restorana gitmek _____
müzeye gitmek _____
televizyon seyretmek _____
müzik dinlemek _____
yüzmek _____
seyahat etmek _____

a Listen to the conversation between Yeşim and Ahmet in which they discuss their plans for the evening, and list the activities you hear mentioned.
b What did they decide to do?
c Listen again and write down the dialogue on a piece of paper.

Rejimdeyim.	*I am on a diet.*
iyi fikir	*good idea*

2 09.15 **Nesrin has a full week ahead of her. She goes through her diary and says what she has to do. Listen to the audio several times. Does she have any free days?**

Ağustos

4 Pazartesi	8 Cuma
8'de tiyatro Banu ile	Boğaz Gezisi Yeşim ve Ahmet ile
5 Salı	**9 Cumartesi**
	2'de Çemberlitaş Hamamı
6 Çarşamba	**10 Pazar**
1.30'da öğle yemeği Gonca ile	Vanessa ile Karagöz ve Hacivat
7 Perşembe	

Now look at the diary and write out next week's entries in Turkish.

3 09.16 **Write the following times in full, then convert them into 12-hour clock format. The first one has been done for you. Listen to them on the audio and repeat them out loud.**

Saat kaç?	24-hour clock	12-hour clock
a 12.30	on iki otuz	yarım
b 15.15	_____	_____
c 08.50	_____	_____
d 04.25	_____	_____
e 18.45	_____	_____

4 Write the following in Turkish.
  a It's five past two.
  b At twenty-five to three.
  c At a quarter past four.
  d It's a quarter to seven.
  e At half past twelve.

5 **Add the -de/-da endings to the following words. Remember to use -de/-da according to the rules of vowel harmony and also to make any necessary consonant changes, e.g., d to t where necessary.**

a sinema
b tiyatro
c iş
d park
e otobüs
f tren

g vapur
h dolmuş
i uçak
j durak
k otel

6 **Reorder the following sentences to form two meaningful dialogues.**

a You are going past a cinema. There is a very good film on which you would like to see. Suggest to your friend that you go and see the film together. Your friend politely refuses the suggestion.

  1 Ne zaman?
  2 Bu cumartesi.
  3 Sinemaya gidelim mi?
  4 Özür dilerim. Meşgulüm.

b You are going past a tea garden in Turkey. It's hot and you are very thirsty. Suggest to your friend that you stop and have a drink. Your friend enthusiastically accepts the suggestion.

  1 Köşede. Kafede.
  2 Nerede?
  3 Çok iyi fikir. Hadi gidelim ve soğuk bir şey içelim.
  4 Çok sıcak, soğuk bir şey içelim mi?

7 **In the left-hand column someone is saying they have a problem or need help. The right-hand column contains offers of help. Match the two together.**

a Program güzel değil.
b Sıkıldım.
c Çok güneş.
d Program sıkıcı.
e Uçak pahalı.

1 Trenle gidelim.
2 Gölgede oturalım.
3 Televizyonu kapatayım mı?
4 Televizyonu kapatalım mı?
5 Müzik koyayım mı?

Reading and writing

1 READING A TIMETABLE

The Bosphorus is the channel between the Black Sea and the Aegean, and it also separates the two continents of Asia and Europe. If you take a boat tour along the Bosphorus in Istanbul, you zigzag between continents!

Read the passage and timetable to get the gist of it. Don't worry if you don't understand every word. Read the passage a couple of times and try to answer the following questions.

1 Where do the boats leave from daily?

2 How many boats leave daily and at what time?

3 At how many places does the boat stop?

4 How long does it stop for at Anadolu Kavağı?

Boğaz gezi vapuru *Boat trips on the Bosphorus*

Vapurumuz Eminönü'nden her gün saat 10.35, 12.00 ve 13.35'te kalkıyor. Özel Boğaz Gezisi Vapuru'muz sırasıyla, Barbaros Hayrettin Paşa, Kanlıca, Emirgan, Yeniköy, Sarıyer, Rumeli Kavağı iskelelerinde duruyor ve Anadolu Kavağı son iskeledir. Vapurumuz her seferinde Anadolu Kavağı'nda 2–3 saat kalmaktadır. Burada çok güzel balık lokantaları vardır.

Ayrıca, cumartesi, pazar ve bayram günleri saat 10.35 ile 13.35 vapurlarımızda canlı müzik vardır.

GİDİŞ				DÖNÜŞ			
EMİNÖNÜ Kalkış	10.35	12.00	13.35	A. KAVAĞI Kalkış	15.00	16.15	17.00
B. H. PAŞA	10.50	12.15	13.50	R. KAVAĞI	15.10	16.00	17.10
KANLICA	11.15	12.40	14.15	SARIYER	15.20	16.25	17.20
EMİRGAN	11.25	12.50	14.25	YENİKÖY	15.35	16.40	17.35
YENİKÖY	11.40	13.05	14.40	EMİRGAN	15.50	16.50	17.50
SARIYER	11.55	13.20	14.55	KANLICA	16.00	17.00	18.00
R. KAVAĞI	12.05	13.45	15.05	B. H. PAS.A	16.25	17.25	18.25
A. KAVAĞI Varış	12.15	13.35	15.15	EMİNÖNÜ Varış	16.35	17.35	18.35

gidiş	*going*	**kalkış**	*leaving*
dönüş	*return*	**varış**	*arriving/arrival*

2 READING A MESSAGE

Here is an authentic environmental message taken from a Turkish newspaper. Write the message in English, then check your answer at the back of the book. To help you find verbs in your dictionary:

▶ take the verb stem,
▶ add **-mek** or **-mak** to form the verb's dictionary form,
▶ now look it up in the dictionary.

> # Yeşili sevelim, ormanları koruyalım.

Speaking

 09.17 Listen to the conversation. Then practise role playing each part. You and a friend are trying to decide what to do this evening.
arkadaş = *friend*

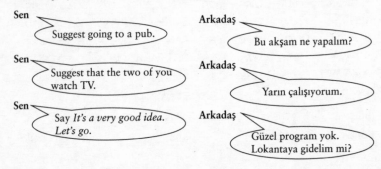

Sen
> Suggest going to a pub.

Arkadaş
> Bu akşam ne yapalım?

Sen
> Suggest that the two of you watch TV.

Arkadaş
> Yarın çalışıyorum.

Sen
> Say *It's a very good idea. Let's go.*

Arkadaş
> Güzel program yok. Lokantaya gidelim mi?

? Test yourself

1 Suggest going to the theatre as there's a good play on.
2 Ask for two return tickets to Istanbul.
3 Say and write out 15.15 in words using the 12-hour clock format.
4 Ask the time.
5 Book a seat at a cinema for this Sunday.

SELF CHECK

I CAN...

- ○ ...make arrangements to go out or suggest doing something.
- ○ ...tell the time.
- ○ ...make reservations for a performance.
- ○ ...buy tickets for public transport.
- ○ ...make, accept or refuse an invitation.

Tatil nasıldı? *How was the holiday?*

In this unit you will learn how to:

▶ *talk about the past, including your experiences and historical facts.*

▶ *write a postcard or an email.*

▶ *have a social chat.*

CEFR *(A2): Can understand and talk about the past, including Turkish historical facts. Can read and write postcards/emails and have a social chat.*

Atatürk, Mustafa Kemal

Mustafa Kemal Atatürk (1881–1938) was the founder of the **Türkiye Cumhuriyeti** (*Turkish Republic*) and as such he is still a key figure in modern Turkey. Under his leadership, Turkish society was transformed radically. Today you will find his statue in every town square and his portrait in schools and offices and on **banknot/kağıt para** (*banknotes*) and stamps.

When Mustafa Kemal was a young man, at the end of the **19'uncu yüzyıl** (*19th century*), Turkey was part of the decaying **Osmanlı İmparatorluğu** (*Ottoman Empire*), which had been ruled for 600 years as an Islamic state by autocratic **padişah/sultan** (*sultans*). Atatürk's vision was to modernise Turkey and he looked towards Western Europe for **model** (*models*) of **demokratik** (*democratic*), **seküler** (*secular*) government.

After the First World War, and the abdication of the last Sultan, Turkey became an autonomous state in 1923 with Atatürk as its leader. Atatürk started his reforms by establishing a parliamentary **demokrasi** (*democracy*), then began a **kültürel** (*cultural*) **devrim** (*revolution*). He wanted to abolish the culture and customs of the Islamic

Ottoman society. He replaced the **Arap alfabesi** (*Arabic alphabet*) with the **Roman alfabesi** (*Roman alphabet*); the Islamic calendar with the western calendar; the Friday 'day of rest' was moved to Sunday. He reformed the dress code for men and women, outlawing the veil and the fez. He reformed the Turkish language. He promoted equality of the sexes, wanting men and women to socialise together. He separated religious affairs from politics, replacing Islamic law with a civil code, while upholding the right of the individual to follow his/her religion of choice.

Today Turkey is a member of NATO, and has for several years been seeking entry to the European Union. Following Atatürk's **kültürel** (*cultural*) and **politik** (*political*) revolution, Turkey is unique in being a secular Islamic country.

1 Who is Atatürk?
2 What did he do?

Vocabulary builder

TATIL HARİKAYDI *THE HOLIDAY WAS WONDERFUL!*

10.01 Listen and repeat. Then complete the missing parts of the Turkish sentences.

H_____. Her gün güneşliydi.	*It was wonderful. It was sunny every day.*
Masmaviydi.	*It was very blue/intense blue/crystal blue.*
Su ılıktı.	*The water was warm.*
Servis çok iyiydi.	*The service was very good.*
Ah, yemekler h_____.	*Ah, the dishes were wonderful.*

NEW EXPRESSIONS

Listen to the words and phrases you will hear in the dialogues. Practise listening and saying the expressions until you feel you have learned them.

Dialogue 1 The holiday was wonderful!

10.02

Bana Yasemin deyin.	*Call me Jasmine.*
Tatiliniz nasıldı?	*How was your holiday?*
bütün	*all*
hiç	*(not) at all*
Hiç yağmur yağmadı.	*It never rained.*

deniz	sea
sakin	calm
masmavi	very blue/intense blue/crystal blue
ılıktı	it was warm
yüzmek	to swim
sandal	rowing boat
kürek çekmek	to row a boat
kumlar	sand
yürümek	to walk
servis	service
çoban salatası	mixed salad (lit. shepherd's salad)
yararlı	good for you
yapmak	to make/to do
dün	yesterday
arkadaşım	my friend
fal bakmak	to read fortunes
gelecek	next
ayırtmak	to book, to reserve
bile	even

Adjectives

10.03 **Listen and repeat these adjectives used in Dialogue 1.**

harika	wonderful
güneşli	sunny
masmavi	very blue/intense blue/crystal blue
ılık	warm
rahat	comfortable
deniz manzaralı	a view of the sea
servis iyi	good service
yararlı	good for you

Dialogue 2 The holiday was a disaster!

10.04

her şey	everything
her şey her şey	absolutely everything
önce	at first
sonra	later
kalmak	to stay
önümüzde	in front of us

inşaat	building site
açık disko	open-air disco
çatal	fork
bıçak	knife
berbat oldu	it is ruined
arı	bee
sokmak	to sting
Arı soktu!	I've been stung by a bee! (lit. A bee has stung me!)

Adjectives

10.05 Listen and repeat these adjectives used in Dialogue 2.

berbat	terrible
kötü	bad
dalgalı	rough
gürültülü	noisy
yakın	near
yüksek	loud/high
sert	hard
bozuk	out of order
lezzetsiz	tasteless
taze	fresh
temiz	clean
yavaş	slow
pahalı	expensive
kötü	bad

Past time expressions

10.06 Listen and repeat. Then complete the missing parts of the Turkish expressions.

dün	yesterday
_____ akşam	yesterday evening
_____ gece	last night
geçen hafta	last week
_____ hafta sonu	last weekend
_____ ay	last month
iki saat önce	two hours ago
geçen yıl/sene	last year

Dialogues

Read the introduction and the gist question for each conversation.
Then listen or read the conversation and answer the questions.

THE HOLIDAY WAS WONDERFUL!

 10.07 *Yasemin's mother is Turkish and her father is English. She was born and brought up in England, and she speaks very good Turkish. She is being interviewed by a Turkish TV* **sunucu** *(presenter) for a holiday programme.*

1 How was her holiday?

Sunucu	İyi günler, Yasemin Hanım.
Yasemin	İyi günler. Bana* Yasemin deyin, lütfen.
Sunucu	Tatiliniz nasıldı?
Yasemin	Harikaydı. Her gün güneşliydi. Bütün hafta hiç yağmur yağmadı.
Sunucu	Deniz?
Yasemin	Sakin ve masmaviydi. Su ılıktı. Her gün yüzdük, sandalda kürek çektik ve kumlarda yürüdük.
Sunucu	Ya otel, otel nasıldı?
Yasemin	Çok rahattı, oda deniz manzaralıydı ve servis çok iyiydi.
Sunucu	Yemekler?
Yasemin	Ah, yemekler harikaydı. Türk yemekleri yapmayı öğreniyorum. Çoban salatası çok yararlı ve lezzetliydi. Dün, Türk kahvesi yaptım ve arkadaşım fal baktı. Her şey çok güzeldi, gelecek tatil için odamı ayırttım bile. Ben burada bir ev almak istiyorum.

*****bana** = *me*

2 What did they do on holiday?

3 What was the food like?

> **TIP**
>
> A **çoban salatası** (*shepherd's salad*) is made from chopped tomato, cucumber, onion and peppers and decorated with fresh chopped parsley. The dressing is just olive oil and vinegar or lemon juice.

2 THE HOLIDAY WAS A DISASTER!

 10.08 *An unhappy holidaymaker is being interviewed by a Turkish TV presenter for a holiday programme.*

1 How was his holiday?

Sunucu	Tatiliniz nasıldı?
Turist	Berbattı. Her şey her şey çok kötüydü.
Sunucu	Hava nasıldı?
Turist	Önce çok sıcaktı, sonra rüzgarlı ve yağmurluydu.
Sunucu	Ya deniz?
Turist	Berbattı. Deniz soğuk ve çok dalgalıydı.
Sunucu	Otel? Nerede kaldınız? Otel nasıldı?
Turist	Otel çok gürültülüydü. Önümüzde bir inşaat vardı, bütün manzarayı kapatıyordu. Açık disko çok yakındı ve müzik çok yüksekti. Yatak sertti, duş bozuktu.
Sunucu	Yemekleri sevdiniz mi?
Turist	Ah, yemekler berbattı, lezzetsizdi. Sebze ve meyveler taze değildi. Çatal, bıçak da hiç temiz değildi. Servis çok yavaştı. Her şey çok pahalıydı ve de çok kötüydü. Kız arkadaşım da beni bıraktı gitti. Tatilim berbat oldu.
(During the interview the tourist is stung by a bee.)	
Turist	Ahh! Arı soktu!

2 How was the weather?

3 Did he like the hotel? Why or why not?

4 How about the food?

Language discovery

1 **Answer these questions about the dialogues. Use Turkish where possible.**
   a How does Yasemin say *it was wonderful*?
   b Name two things which were wonderful.
   c How does the tourist say *the weather was at first too hot, then windy and rainy*?
   d How does he say *the food was terrible*?

2 **Practise the dialogues using your name and the names of people you know.**

3 Match the questions and answers. Then check with the dialogues. There are two answers for each question.

a	Tatiliniz nasıldı?	**1**	Harikaydı.
b	Hava nasıldı?	**2**	Önce çok sıcak, sonra rüzgarlı ve yağmurluydu.
c	Deniz?	**3**	Berbattı.
d	Otel nasıldı?	**4**	Çok rahattı, oda deniz manzaralıydı ve servis çok iyiydi.
e	Yemekler?	**5**	Berbattı, lezzetsizdi. Sebze ve meyveler taze değildi.
		6	Harikaydı. Her gün güneşliydi.
		7	Çok gürültülüydü. Yatak sertti, duş bozuktu.
		8	Sakin ve masmaviydi. Su ılıktı.
		9	Harikaydı.
		10	Berbattı. Soğuk ve dalgalıydı.

4 Look at the dialogues. Complete these sentences. Notice how the endings change according to the vowel harmony *-dı (-di, -du, -dü)*.

a Tatiliniz nasıl_____?

b Harika_____.

c Oda deniz manzaralı_____.

d Arkadaşım fal bak_____.

e Kız arkadaşım da beni bırakıp git_____.

Go further

1 USING THE PAST TENSE *-DI (-Dİ, -DU, -DÜ)*

To talk about the past, you need to learn just the one simple past tense in Turkish. You may have noticed that you use the same form to talk about things which happened and which have happened.

In Turkish you add the past tense endings **-di** (**-dı**, **-du**, **-dü**) to nouns, adjectives and adverbs to describe how things were. The ending is added before the verb *to be*/personal ending. Here are some examples:

The past form of *to be*

Present tense		Past tense	
(ben)	**Rahatım.** *I am comfortable.*	**Rahattım.**[1] *I was comfortable.*	
(sen)	**Rahatsın.**	**Rahattın.**	
(o)	**Rahat.**	**Rahattı.**	
(biz)	**Rahatız.**	**Rahattık.**	
(siz)	**Rahatsınız.**	**Rahattınız.**	
(onlar)	**Rahatlar.**	**Rahattılar.** or **Rahatlardı.**	
(ben)	**İyiyim.**[2] *I'm fine/good.*	**İyiydim.** *I was fine/good.*	
(sen)	**İyisin.**	**İyiydin.**	
(o)	**İyi.**	**İyiydi.**	
(biz)	**İyiyiz.**	**İyiydik.**	
(siz)	**İyisiniz.**	**İyiydiniz.**	
(onlar)	**İyiler.**	**İyiydiler.** or **İyilerdi.**	

[1] Remember, **d** becomes **t** after **t** as in **rahattım**.

[2] Remember, buffer **y** is added between vowels, as in **iyiyim** and **iyiydim**.

You say *was not* or *were not* by using the word **değil** with the same endings used above. For example:

Negatives in the present tense		Negatives in the past tense	
(ben)	**İyi değilim.** *I'm not well.*	(ben)	**İyi değildim.** *I wasn't well.*
(sen)	**İyi değilsin.**	(sen)	**İyi değildin.**
(o)	**İyi değil.**	(o)	**İyi değildi.**
(biz)	**İyi değiliz.**	(biz)	**İyi değildik.**
(siz)	**İyi değilsiniz.**	(siz)	**İyi değildiniz.**
(onlar)	**İyi değiller.**	(onlar)	**İyi değillerdi.** or **değildiler.**

You use **mı**, **mi**, **mu** or **mü** to make the sentence a question.

Questions in the present tense	Questions in the past tense
Harika mıyım? *Am I wonderful?*	**Harika mıydım?** *Was I wonderful?*
Harika mısın?	**Harika mıydın?**
Harika mı?	**Harika mıydı?**
Harika mıyız?	**Harika mıydık?**
Harika mısınız?	**Harika mıydınız?**
Harikalar mı?/Onlar harika mı?	**Harikalar mıydı?/(Harika mıydılar?)**

To make a verb in the past tense negative (*did not*), add **-me** or **-ma** onto the stem of the verb before the **-di** ending and the personal ending.

(ben)	**Sevmedim.**	**Almadım.**	**Durmadım.**	**Yüzmedim.**
(sen)	**Sevmedin.**	**Almadın.**	**Durmadın.**	**Yüzmedin.**
(o)	**Sevmedi.**	**Almadı.**	**Durmadı.**	**Yüzmedi.**
(biz)	**Sevmedik.**	**Almadık.**	**Durmadık.**	**Yüzmedik.**
(siz)	**Sevmediniz.**	**Almadınız.**	**Durmadınız.**	**Yüzmediniz.**
(onlar)	**Sevmediler.**	**Almadılar.**	**Durmadılar.**	**Yüzmediler.**

To make a verb in the past tense into a question (*did I ...?*) add **mı**, **mi**, **mu** or **mü** after the **di** ending and the personal ending.

(ben)	**Sevdim mi?**	**Aldım mı?**	**Durdum mu?**	**Yüzdüm mü?**
(sen)	**Sevdin mi?**	**Aldın mı?**	**Durdun mu?**	**Yüzdün mü?**
(o)	**Sevdi mi?**	**Aldı mı?**	**Durdu mu?**	**Yüzdü mü?**
(biz)	**Sevdik mi?**	**Aldık mı?**	**Durduk mu?**	**Yüzdük mü?**
(siz)	**Sevdiniz mi?**	**Aldınız mı?**	**Durdunuz mu?**	**Yüzdünüz mü?**
(onlar)	**Sevdiler mi?**	**Aldılar mı?**	**Durdular mı?**	**Yüzdüler mi?**

2 USING THE PAST TENSE

Turkish does not have an equivalent of the English tense *have done* (present perfect). Instead, you often use the past tense, for example:

Arı soktu!	*A bee has stung me!*
Hiç ayran içtin mi?	*Have you ever drunk 'ayran'?*
İstanbul'a hiç gitmedim.	*I haven't been to Istanbul.*
Ayasofya'ya gittin mi?	*Have you been to St Sophia?*

Where English uses the present tense to signify something ongoing, note that Turkish sometimes uses the past tense to signify this. In conversations, you are likely to hear the following:

Sentence	Literal translation	Meaning
Efendim, anlamadım.	*Pardon, I didn't understand you.*	*I don't understand you.*
Sıkıldım.	*I was bored.*	*I'm bored.*
Acıktım.	*I was hungry.*	*I'm hungry.*
Susadım.	*I was thirsty.*	*I'm thirsty.*
Yoruldum.	*I got tired.*	*I'm tired.*
Yolumu kaybettim.	*I lost my way.*	*I'm lost.*
Geç kaldım.	*I was late.*	*I'm late.*
Geldim.	*I came.*	*I'm coming. I'll be right there.*
Memnun oldum.	*I became glad.*	*I'm glad.*

3 WORDS SIMILAR TO ENGLISH

Here are some cognates related to this unit's theme: **modern Türkiye** (*modern Turkey*), **bankanot** (*banknotes*), **model** (*model*) of **demokratik** (*democratic*), **seküler** (*secular*), **demokrasi** (*democracy*), **kültürel** (*cultural*), **Arap alfabesi** (*Arabic alphabet*), **Roman alfabesi** (*Roman alphabet*), **NATO** (*NATO*), **politik** (*political*), **otel** (*hotel*), **disko** (*disco*), **müzik** (*music*), **konser** (*concert*), **müzikal** (*musical*), **Asya** (*Asia*), **Osmanlılar** (*Ottomans*), **Avrupa** (*Europe*), **kervansaray** (*caravanserai*). Practise saying them out loud in Turkish.

Practice

Complete the following with the year or the written form. The first one is done for you.

We write	We say
a 1071	bin yetmiş bir
b 1453	
c	bin dokuz yüz yirmi
d 1935	
e	bin dokuz yüz yetmiş yedi
f 2014	

Listening

 10.09 Guess who? Listen to this biography of a famous American. Notice the use of the past tense. Guess this person's identity then answer the questions. Listen as many times as you need before looking at the transcript in the back of the book.

doğmak	*to be born*
8 Ocak 1935'te	*on the 8th January 1935*
ilk	*first*
kez	*time*
plak	*record*
anlaşmak	*to sign a contract*
TV'ye çıkmak	*to be on TV*
askerlik	*military service*
askerliğini yaptı	*did his military service*
...ile evlenmek	*to get married to...*
boşanmak	*to divorce*
arası	*between*
konser vermek	*to give a concert*
ölmek	*to die*
16 Ağustos 1977'de	*on the 16th August 1977*
...'den fazla	*more than...*
müzikal	*musical*
oynamak	*to act*
ödül	*award*
altın	*gold*
platin	*platinum*
kral	*king*

1 Kim?

2 Askerlik yaptı mı?

3 Kimle evlendi?

4 Yakışıklı mıydı?

5 Mesleği neydi?

6 Ünlü müydü?

7 Siz onu hiç dinlediniz mi?

Speaking

10.10 **Listen to the conversation. Then practise role playing each part.**

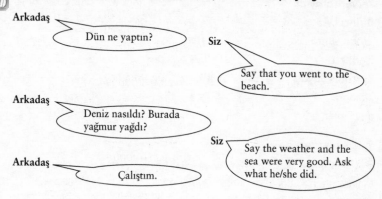

Arkadaş: Dün ne yaptın?

Siz: Say that you went to the beach.

Arkadaş: Deniz nasıldı? Burada yağmur yağdı?

Siz: Say the weather and the sea were very good. Ask what he/she did.

Arkadaş: Çalıştım.

Reading

Read the brief passage about Turkish history below and answer the questions. You do not need to know every word to be able to understand the passage. However, we have given you key words and there is a translation of the passage in the Answer key.

tarih	history
Türk tarihi	Turkish history
Anadolu	Anatolia
Orta Asya	Central Asia
Selçuk Türkleri	Seljuk
Malazgirt	Manzikert (the name of a town)
girdi	entered
yayıldı	spread
Osman Bey	Osman (the head of the Ottoman clan)
Bursa'ya kadar	as far as Bursa
Fatih Sultan Mehmet	Sultan Mehmet the conqueror
aldı	conquered, took
Osmanlılar	Ottomans
Orta Avrupa	Central Europe

durdular	*stopped*
köprüler	*bridges*
kervansaraylar	*caravanserai* (inns with large courtyards)
Birinci Dünya Savaşı	*First World War*
...'dan sonra	*after...*
işgal ettiler	*they occupied*
Kurtuluş Savaşı	*War of Independence*
kazandı	*won*
devrimler	*reforms*

Türk tarihi *Turkish history*

Türkler, Anadolu'ya Orta Asya'dan geldiler. Selçuk Türkleri 1071'de[1] doğuda Malazgirt'ten Anadolu'ya girdi ve batıya yayıldı. Osman Bey, Bursa'ya kadar geldi, sonra Bursa başkent oldu. 1453'te[2] Fatih Sultan Mehmet, Konstantinapol'u[3] aldı ve Osmanlı başkenti yaptı. Osmanlılar, Orta Avrupa'da Viyana'da durdular. Osmanlılar, Avrupa ve Anadolu'da çok güzel camiler, köprüler ve kervansaraylar yaptılar. Birinci Dünya Savaşı'ndan sonra İngiliz, Fransız, İtalyan ve Yunanlılar Türkiye'yi işgal ettiler. Atatürk, Kurtuluş Savaşı'nı kazandı. Türkiye, Cumhuriyet oldu. Ankara, başkent oldu. Atatürk ilk Türk Cumhurbaşkanı oldu ve çok devrimler yaptı.

[1] **1071'de** = *in 1071*

[2] **1453'te** = *in 1453*

[3] **Kostantinapol** = *Constantinople* (today's Istanbul)

1 Why is Sultan Mehmet important?

2 What is the Ottomans' contribution to the architecture of Europe and Anatolia?

3 According to the passage, in which three ways did Atatürk contribute to the history of Turkey?

Turkish writers

Some contemporary Turkish writers, including Ayşe Kulin, Buket Uzuner and Zülfü Livanelli, are prolific and popular. Books by all three authors have been translated into English.

If you are interested in Turkish history, *Atatürk* by Andrew Mango and *Turkey: A Short History* by Norman Stone are among the best history books written about Turkey. Halil İnalcık is considered an expert historian on Ottoman history.

Writing

1 Su is on holiday in Turkey. She stayed on a holiday island for a week then came to Istanbul where she wrote this postcard. Pay particular attention to her use of tenses. Then answer the questions.

Sevgili Anneciğim,

Tatil harika geçiyor. Her sabah simit yiyorum. Üç kere deveye bindim. Henüz rakı içmedim. Hava her gün güneşli. Bir hafta adada kaldık, şimdi İstanbul'dayız. Dün Topkapı'ya gittik ama henüz Ayasofya'yı gezmedik. Sana bir kilo lokum aldım. On gündür tavla öğreniyorum. Çok mutluyum. Yakında görüşürüz.

Sevgilerimle

Su

xx

---

a Su hiç rakı içti mi?

b Su şimdi adada mı?

c Su, Ayasofya'yı gezdi mi?

2 Now write a similar postcard or an email to a friend in Turkey and describe your recent holiday. Use the postcard as a model.

Test yourself

1 **10.11** You are a TV presenter who asked two holidaymakers (one happy, one unhappy) the same questions. Their answers got muddled up by the computer. Try to work out the answer each gave to each question. Then listen and check your answers.

a İyi günler.	**1** İyi günler.
b Tatiliniz nasıldı?	**2** Çok iyiydi.
c Hava nasıldı?	**3** Yemekler berbattı, lezzetsizdi.
d Otel nasıldı?	**4** Otel çok gürültülüydü.
e Yemekler nasıldı?	**5** Çok rüzgarlı ve yağmurluydu.
	6 Her gün güneşliydi.
	7 Çok rahattı, oda deniz manzaralıydı.
	8 Çok kötüydü.
	9 Yemekler harikaydı.
	10 İyi günler.

2 Here are four situations where A says what he/she did and B asks questions about it. Choose the best follow-up question for each situation.

a A: Dün akşam sinemaya gittim.	**1**	B: Denizde mi, havuzda mı?
b A: Geçen pazar pideciye gittik.	**2**	B: Hangi filmi gördün?
c A: Geçen hafta kitap aldım.	**3**	B: Hangi kitabı aldın?
d A: Hafta sonunda yüzdüm.	**4**	B: Kimle gittin?

3 The verbs in the following list are in the dictionary (infinitive) form. Give their past forms. The first one has been done for you.

	ben	sen o	o
a doğmak	doğdum	doğdun	doğdu
b anlaşmak			
c TV'ye çıkmak			
d plak yapmak			
e evlenmek			
f boşanmak			
g konser vermek			
h oynamak			

	ben	sen o	o
i ödül almak			
j ölmek			

4 Match the Turkish words with their English meanings.

a Türkiye   1 democratic
b modern   2 cultural
c demokratik   3 political
d seküler   4 service
e kültürel   5 disco
f politik   6 music
g servis   7 concert
h disko   8 Turkey
i müzik   9 secular
j konser   10 modern

5 Complete the sentences. The following passage, taken from earlier in the unit, needs to have the correct verb endings inserted. They should all be in the past tense.

Türk tarihi

Türkler, Anadolu'ya Orta Asya'dan **1** gel_____. Selçuk Türkleri 1071'de doğuda Malazgirt'ten Anadolu'ya **2** gir_____ ve batıya **3** yayıl_____. Osman Bey, Bursa'ya kadar **4** gel_____, sonra Bursa başkent **5** ol_____. 1453'te Fatih Sultan Mehmet, Konstantinapol'u **6** al_____ ve Osmanlı başkenti **7** yap_____. Osmanlılar, Orta Avrupa'da Viyana'da **8** dur_____. Osmanlılar, Avrupa ve Anadolu'da çok güzel camiler, köprüler ve kervansaraylar **9** yap_____. Birinci Dünya Savaşı'ndan sonra İngiliz, Fransız, İtalyan ve Yunanlılar Türkiye'yi işgal **10** et_____. Atatürk, Kurtuluş Savaşı'nı **11** kazan_____. Türkiye Cumhuriyet **12** ol_____. Ankara, başkent **13** ol_____. Atatürk ilk Türk Cumhurbaşkanı **14** ol_____ ve çok devrimler **15** yap_____.

6 Ask someone if he/she has done each of these things. Remember that Turkish uses the past tense for this. Write or say your questions in Turkish.

Example: **Hiç rakı içtin mi?** *Have you ever drunk raki?*

a	tavla oynamak	*to play backgammon*
b	nargile içmek	*to smoke a hookah*
c	simit yemek	*to eat simit (bread in the shape of a ring)*
d	deveye binmek	*to ride a camel*
e	çamur banyosu yapmak	*to have a mud bath*
f	Ayasofya'yı gezmek	*to visit St Sophia*
g	hamama gitmek	*to go to a Turkish bath*
h	Karagöz ve Hacivat'ı seyretmek	*to watch Karagöz and Hacivat (traditional puppet show)*

7 Look at the pictures and describe last week's weather. Use a dictionary if needed. The first one is done for you.

a

pazartesi   Pazartesi güneşliydi.

b

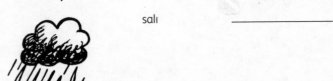

salı   _____

c çarşamba _____

d perşembe _____

e cuma _____

f cumartesi _____

g pazar _____

8 Answer the questions about yourself. Write or say your answers in Turkish if possible.

  a Dün akşam neredeydin?
  b Dün akşam ne yaptın?
  c Geçen hafta sonu evde miydin?
  d Geçen pazar ne yaptın?
  e Hiç Türkçe film seyrettin mi?
  f Hiç Efes'e gittin mi?
  g Hiç Boğaz'da vapurla gezdin mi?
  h Hiç Türkçe müzik dinlediniz mi?

ev	*house*
seyretmek	*to watch*
Efes	*Ephesus*
Boğaz	*the Bosphorus*
dinlemek	*to listen*

9 10.12 Listen and answer the following questions orally or in writing or both.

  1 Ask someone how their holiday was.
  2 Explain that your holiday was awful and everything went wrong.
  3 Say that you have been to a Turkish bath.
  4 Say that you have not had a mud bath.
  5 Ask someone if they have ridden a camel.

SELF CHECK

I CAN...

○ ... talk about the past, including my experiences and historical facts.

○ ... write a postcard or an email.

○ ... have a social chat.

Bravo! Tebrikler! *Congratulations!* You have completed *Get started in Turkish*. You should be able to handle most everyday situations on a visit to Turkey and to communicate with Turkish people sufficiently to make friends. If you would like to extend your ability so that you can develop your confidence and fluency and cope in the language, whether for social or business purposes, why not take your Turkish a step further with the *Complete Turkish* course?

I hope that working your way through *Get started in Turkish* has been an enjoyable learning experience.

İyi şanslar!   Asuman Çelen Pollard

Answer key

UNIT 1

Greeting people in Turkey
1 bir Türk; **2** bir Müslüman

Vocabulary builder
Greetings: İyi; İyi.
Times of the day: a Günydın or Merhaba/Selam; **b** İyi akşamlar.

Dialogue 1
1 İyi akşamlar; **2** Şarap

Dialogue 2
1 informal; **2** Evet

Dialogue 3
1 Ülkü and Banu; **2** Çok güzel; **3** Bahadır Bey

Dialogue 4
1 She uses 'Bey' and 'siz'.; **2** İyi; **3** 'Hoşça kalın' and 'İyi geceler'.

Language discovery
1 a İyi akşamlar; **b** şarap & bira; **c** Evet, çok güzel.; **d** Güle güle, Banu.
3 a/5; b/3; c/2; d/1; e/4
4 a sınız; **b** sın
5 a Çay güzel, değil mi?; **b** Güzel bir çay, değil mi?; **c** Çok güzel bir gece, değil mi?

Practice
1 e/1; c/2; b/3; d/4; a/5; f/6
2 a Bey; **b** Hanım
3 a/4; b/1; c/2; d/3
4 a a party; **b** a beer; **c** a (glass of) wine
5 a değil; **b** değil mi; **c** değil; **d** değil mi; **e** değil; **f** değil mi
6 a değil mi?, değil mi; **b** değil mi? **c** değil mi?

Pronunciation
2 0 = sıfır; 1 = bir; 2 = iki; 3 = üç; 4 = dört; 5 = beş; 6 = altı; 7 = yedi; 8 = sekiz; 9 = dokuz; 10 = on

Speaking
Gökhan: Merhaba; Sema.; Gökhan: İyiyim. Sen nasılsın? Gökhan: Hoşça kal; Sema ;Gökhan; Görüşürüz.

Reading and writing

1 **a** from Ayşe; **b** to Ahmet; **c** Akşama

3 **a** morning; **b** evening

Test yourself

1 **a** Merhaba./Selam.; **b** Merhaba./Selam./Günaydın.; **c** Günaydın./İyi günler.

2 İyi geceler.

3 Hoşça kal./Hoşça kalın.

4 Güle güle./Hoşça kal./Hoşça kalın.

5 **a** Merhaba; **b** ben

6 **a** 5; **b** 10; **c** 1; **d** 9; **e** 3; **f** 7; **g** 4; **h** 2; **i** 6; **j** 8; **k** 0

7 **a** 7; **b** 2; **c** 1; **d** 5; **e** 8; **f** 2; **g** 3; **h** 10; **i** 1

8

M	E	R	H	A	B	A	B	İ	R
N	R	S	A	V	E	Z	A	K	T
A	C	İ	N	O	Y	D	O	İ	R
S	L	A	I	N	P	J	S	T	V
I	R	C	M	P	O	U	S	E	N
L	F	N	O	P	Z	H	İ	B	J
S	A	L	T	İ	R	S	Z	J	C
I	B	N	T	R	P	S	O	V	J
N	İ	Y	İ	Y	İ	M	R	T	U
P	S	I	R	G	D	Ç	F	O	N

9 **a** Merhaba.; **b** Hoşça kal.; **c** İyi geceler.; **d** Nasılsınız?; **e** Nasılsın?

UNIT 2

Having a drink in Turkey

1 Bir Türk kahvesi, lütfen.; 2 Bir çay, lütfen.

Vocabulary builder

bardak; bardak

Dialogue 1

1 Bir çay; bir sütlü Nescafé; 2 çay, bira, su, Nescafé, süt; 3 sütlü

Dialogue 2

1 şekerli ve şekersiz kahve, ayran ve peynirli toast; 2 şekerli ve sade; 3 çok güzel;

Dialogue 3

1 kırmızı şarap, rakı, fıstık, karışık meyve ve beyaz peynir; 2 kırmızı şarap; 3 beyaz peynir

Language discovery

1 iyi aks͵amlar iyi geceler selamlar tebrikler mutlu yıllar mutlu bayramlar iyi s͵anslar iyi yolculuklar iyi günler renkli rüyalar mutlu Noeller

2 iyi aks͵amlar iyi geceler selamlar tebrikler mutlu yıllar mutlu bayramlar iyi s͵anslar iyi yolculuklar iyi günler renkli rüyalar mutlu Noeller

3 **a** kahveler; **b** tostlar; **c** çaylar; **d** sütler

Go further

2 Colours

1 coffee-coloured; **2** wine-coloured; **3** turquoise blue

Practice

1 **a** bira; **b** çay; **c** Nescafe; **d** ayran; **e** şarap

3 **a** çaylar; **b** rakılar; **c** tostlar; **d** teşekkürler; **e** biralar; **f** içecekler

4 **a** sarı; **b** beyaz; **c** mavi; **d** kırmızı

5 **a** turuncu; **b** yeşil; **c** gri; **d** pembe; **e** mor

6 **a** yanlış; **b** yanlış; **c** doğru; **d** doğru; **e** yanlış

7 **a** 0; **b** 57; **c** 11; **d** 35; **e** 23; **f** 46; **g** 60

Speaking

Bir bardak çay, lütfen.; Bir peynirli bir tost, lütfen.; Teşekkürler.

Test yourself

1 Garson.; **2** Bir şekerli kahve, lütfen. or Bir şekersiz kahve, lütfen. or Bir sade kahve, lütfen.; **3** Sütlü Nescafe, lütfen.; **4** Bir bardak çay, lütfen.; **5** Bir bardak kırmızı ve bir bardak beyaz şarap, lütfen.

UNIT 3

Accommodation in Turkey

1 Otel var mı?; **2** pansiyon

Vocabulary builder

bu; bu; Bu; bu

Dialogue 1

1 Kalacak yerler listesi; **2** Yeşil Ev; **3** Otel

Dialogue 2

1 Oda; **2** üç gece; **3** Evet, dahil.

Dialogue 3

1 Kamp; **2** Telefon var mı acaba?; **3** Evet

Dialogue 4

1 Çok meşgulüz.; **2** Araba parkı, telefon, yüzme havuzu, restoran ve tuvaletler

Language discovery

1 **a** Nasıl yazılır, lütfen?; **b** Boş oda var mı?; **c** İki kişilik çadır var mı?; **d** Meşgulüz.

2 Yediyüzelliiki elliiki sıfıraltı

3 Beware of the dog!

Go further

6 This, that

by adding **nlar** at the end

8 This/That place

bu-bura, şu-şura, o-ora

10 Borrowed words

otel = hotel, pansiyon = B&B, resepsiyon = reception, liste = list, kamp = campsite, telefon = telephone, duş = shower, pasaport = passport, balkon = balcony, adres = address, elektrik = electricity, restoran = restaurant, kart = cart, plaj = beach, park = park, tuvalet = toilet, bungalov = bungalow

Practice

1 **a** ikiyüzkırkaltı elli otuzbeş; **b** ikiyüzatmışiki sıfırbir otuzyedi; **c** altıyüzondört onüç otuzüç; **d** yediyüzonyedi yirmiiki yirmidört; **e** sekizyüzdoksanaltı otuzaltı otuzaltı; **f** üçyüzonbir kırksekiz elliyedi

2 **a** 531; **b** 444; **c** 6,755; **d** 1,001; **e** 3,033; **f** 916; **g** 7,814; **h** 4,000

3 **a**/5; **b**/1; **c**/6; **d**/2; **e**/3; **f**/4

4 **a** global system for mobile communication; **b** address; **c** passport number

5 e; a; b; d; c; f; g

Speaking

Siz: Hoş bulduk. Boş oda var mı?; Tek kişilik bir oda, lütfen.; Duş var mı?; Beş gece.; Teşekkürler.

Test yourself

1 Duşlu bir oda, lütfen. 2 Boş oda var mı? 3 Kahvaltı dahil mi? 4 Nasıl yazılır? 5 Bu, şu, o

UNIT 4

Turkish cuisine

1 Ekmek, su; 2 Etsiz yemek ne var?

Vocabulary builder

bahçede; kahvaltıda; masada; burada; sağda.

Dialogue 1

1 Türk kahvaltısı; 2 Çok güzel.; 3 Rafadan

Dialogue 2

1 They look at the balık mönü. or They order kalkan, levrek, barbunya, lüfer.; 2 Vişne suyu; 3 Asuman

Dialogue 3
1 öğlen köfte; **2** bira; **3** karışık salata

Language discovery
1 **a** Bizim için Türk kahvaltısı, lütfen.; **b** Kahvaltıda neler var.; **c** Garson, hesap, lütfen.; **d** Burada, sağda, efendim.; **e** Bira soğuk mu?
2 **a** Bahçede...; **b** Kahvaltıda...; **c** Vowel harmony determines the ending.

Go further
3 Questions with **mı**, **mi**, **mu** or **mü**
1 Üzüm mü?; **2** Çay var mı?; **3** Soğuk mu?; **4** Köfte çok lezzetli, değil mi?

Practice
1 çay; zeytin; tereyağı; şeker; iki yumurta; reçel ve beyaz peynir
2 **a** mi?; **b** mi?; **c** mi?; **d** mu?; **e** mu?; **f** mü?
3 **a** 1; **d** 2; **b** 3; **e** 4; **c** 5; **f** 6
4 **a** çay; **b** balık; **c** salata; **d** ekmek
5 **a** Evet, İstanbul'da.; **b** Evet, soğuk.; **c** Evet, et.; **d** Evet, ucuz.; **e** Hayır, meyve.; **f** Hayır, lezzetsiz.; **g** Hayır, alkollü değil.; **h** Evet, tatlı.; **i** Evet, siyah.; **j** Evet; taze.
6 **a** 4; **b** 3; **c** 6; **d** 2; **e** 1; **f** 5
7 **a** Açık havada; **b** Burada; **c** mu?; masada; **d** mı?; **e** mu?

Speaking
Bir kıymalı pide ve bir lahmacun, lütfen.; Bir ayran, bir kola, lütfen.

Reading
1 Çok lezzetli.; **2** Yum, yum.

Test yourself
1 Bir kahve, tereyağı, ekmek, sosis ve yumurta, lütfen.; **2** Balık tava ve yeşil salata, lütfen.; **3** Bir büyük beyaz şarap, lütfen.; **4** İki porsiyon köfte ve pilav, lütfen. **5** Bira soğuk mu?

UNIT 5

Asking for directions
1 Affedersiniz, tuvaletler nerede?; **2** It means 'tuvalet'.

Vocabulary builder
Cognates: bank; passport; control; taxi; kilometre; museum; harem; card

Dialogue 1
1 banka, tuvaletler, taksiler; **2 a** evet; **b** hayır; **c** evet

Dialogue 2
1 Topkapı Müzesi; **2** 9'dan 5'e kadar; **3** Düz gidin, orada.

Dialogue 3

1 Birinci; **2** Bodrum'dan Ören'e; **3** Sahilde, merkezde.

Language discovery

1 **a** excuse me; **b** I'm sorry; **c** I wonder; **d** pardon; **e** not at all; **f** here you are; **g** not at all

Practice

1 **a** 3; **b** 4; **c** 1; **d** 2

2 **a** 3; **b** 4; **c** 2; **d** 5; **e** 1

3 **a** Here you are.; **b** On me.; **c** Do not disturb!; **d** Excuse me.; **e** I am sorry.; **f** I do not know.; **g** Thanks.; **h** Not at all.

4 **a** 1; **b** 3; **c** 5; **d** 6; **e** 4; **f** 2

5 **a** 454 km; **b** 815 km; **c** 325 km; **d** 404 km; **e** 666km; **f** 814 km; **g** 750 km; **h** 565 km; **i** 1,079 km; **j** 926 km

6 **a** Marmaris'ten Çiftlik'e; **b** Çiftlik'ten Bozukkale'ye; **c** Bozukkale'den Aktur'a Aktur'dan Datça'ya; **d** Datça'dan Knidos'a; **e** Knidos'tan Bodrum'a

Speaking

Siz: Afedersiniz, müze nerde, acaba?; Çok teşekkür ederim.

Test yourself

1 Afedersiniz, banka nerede, acaba?; **2** Afedersiniz taksiler nerede, acaba?; **3** Düz gidin ve köşede sağa dönün, lütfen.; **4** Müze ne zaman açık?; **5** İki bilet, lütfen.

UNIT 6

Special days

1 Turkish is May the 2nd; British English is 2nd of May. **2** It involves sharing food, in this case by sacrificing an animal such as a sheep or goat.

Vocabulary builder

Travel: en sıcak; güneşli

Dialogue 1

1 Evet, 28 derece; **2** İstanbul, 23 derece; **3** Pazartesi, Çarşamba, Cuma, Cumartesi ve Pazar

Dialogue 2

1 Sevdikleri şeyleri. (They're talking about the things they like.); **2** Cem ve Gökhan futbol, basketbol, voleybol ve tenis seviyor. Vanessa denizi ve dansı ve günlük gezileri seviyor; **3** cikolatalı ve limonlu

Language discovery

1 **a** Çocuklar da denizi ve kumu seviyor; **b** Kırlarda kır çiçekleri çok çeşitli ve güzeldir; **c** Çikolatalı, sade, meyveli, limonlu ve karışık

Go further

1 Formal -dır (-dir, -dur, -dür)

1 b; **2** c; **3** d; **4** a

3 Comparatives and superlatives

adjective	comparative	superlative
sıcak	daha sıcak	en sıcak
çok	daha çok	en çok
ılık	daha ılık	en ılık
serin	daha serin	en serin
soğuk	daha soğuk	en soğuk

6 The ending -me, -ma

Orada durma. (*Don't stay there.*)

Practice

1 a Batıda; **b** Kuzey batıda; **c** Ortada; **d** Doğuda; **e** Güney batıda;
f Kuzeyde; **g** Güneyde; **h** Güneyde; **i** Güney batıda

2 a 4 güneşsiz; **b** 2 bulutsuz; **c** 1 yağmursuz; **d** 3 karsız; **e** 6 sissiz; **f** 7; **g** 5

3 Dursun en kısa boylu.

4 a ağustos; **b** eylül; **c** ekim; **d** haziran; **e** temmuz; **f** şubat

5 a 5; **b** 6; **c** 3; **d** 2; **e** 4; **f** 1

Speaking

Siz: Temmuzda Alanya'da hava nasıl? Alanya'ya uçak var mı? Perşembe için yer var mı? Bir kişi için. / Bir kişilik.

Reading and writing

1 Türkiye'de mevsimler ve iklim; Seasons and climate in Turkey. **2** Hayır; farklı. No, it's different.

Test yourself

1 Yazın hiç yağmur yok. **2** İlkbaharda yağmur var/yağmurlu. **3** Temmuz şubattan daha sıcaktır. **4** En çok dans etmeyi ve voleybolu seviyorum. **5** Bodrum'a hangi günler uçak var?

UNIT 7

Addressing people

Words used for women: Hanım, Hanımefendi, abla, teyze, anne, nene; Words used for men: Bey, Beyefendi, amca, abi, baba, dede.

Vocabulary builder

Almanca; İspanyolca; Bulgarca.

Dialogue 1

1 Bonnlu and ve Leeds'li Leeds'li; **2** 6 İngilizce

Dialogue 2

1 Ayda Türk; Susie Londralı; **2** kimse nobody; **3** Cem uzun boylu, esmer, siyah saçlı, siyah gözlü, çok yakışıklı. Çok akıllı ve iyi bir insane.

Dialogue 3

1 Abla; **2** İyi; **3** İyi

Dialogue 4

1 Informally; they use 'merhaba' and the 'send' form; **2** İyi

Language discovery

1 **a** Almanım; **b** Eeşim Türk. **c** Evet, haklısınız.

2 (Dialogue numbers in brackets) **a** Nerelisin? (1); evli misin? (2); **b** İngilizim (1); öğrenciyim (2); değilim (2); **c** nerelisiniz? (1); **d** Almanım (1); Londralı'yım (2); çalışkanım (2); nişanlıyım (2); bekarım (2); yaşındayım (2); **e** Bonn'luyum (1); doktorum (2); **f** şanslıyız (1); arkadaşız (2); **g** haklısınız (1); **h** Türk müsün? (2); **i** akıllısın (2)

Practice

1 **a** 3; **b** 4; **c** 8; **d** 1; **e** 7; **f** 9; **g** 2; **h** 5; **i** 6

2 **a** Ben İngilizim ama eşim Türk. **b** Hayır, İngilizim. **c** Çok akıllı değilim ama çok çalışkanım. **d** Nişanlın yakışıklı mı? **e** Gonca, Abla siz misiniz?

3 **a** saçlı; **b** gözlü; **c** boylu; **d** saçlı, gözlü; **e** Yeşilli

4 **a** yakışıklı; **b** güzel; **c** akıllı; **d** çalışkan; **e** Türkçe; **f** Türkiye; **g** işsiz; **h** kolay; **i** değil mi; **j** gramer

5 **a** 10; **b** 9; **c** 6; **d** 8; **e** 3; **f** 7; **g** 5; **h** 2; **i** 1; **j** 4

6 **a** Türkiye'de. **b** Fransa'da. **c** Evet, İngiltere'de. **d** Amerika'da. **e** Evet Rusya'da.

Listening

Name	Nationality	Job	Marital status	Age	Home town
Bülent	Turkish	doctor	—	—	İzmir
Lucy	American	model	single	24	
Trish Webb	English	teacher	single	—	Birmingham
Philippe	French	footballer	single	21	Paris
Ülkü Gezer	Turkish	photographer	married	43	Istanbul
June	Australian	flight attendant	married	—	Sydney

Speaking

Siz: 1 Merhaba. **2** Hayır, Amerikalı değilim; İngilizim. **3** Evet, bir Türk'le evliyim. **4** Mühendisim. **5** Siz de çok akıllısınız.

Reading and writing

1 a İstanbullu; **b** Mühendis; **c** Siyah saçlı; siyah gözlü ve uzun boylu. **d** Hayır, bekar.

Test yourself

1 Amerikalı mısınız? **2** Kaç yaşındasınız? **3** Milliyetiniz ne? **4** Evliyim. **5** Bekar mısınız?

UNIT 8

Shopping in Turkey

1 It is very different. **2** The Mısır Çarşısı (Egyptian Bazaar) gets its name from the ancient tradition of trade with Egypt in coffee, spices, etc.

Vocabulary builder

almak = to buy

Dialogue 1

1 Alışveriş (shopping) yapmak istiyorlar. **2** Ben hediye almak istiyor. **3** Kapalı Çarşı'ya gitmek istiyorlar/gidiyorlar.

Dialogue 2

1 Deri çanta almak istiyor. **2** Evet

Dialogue 3

1 Köftelik baharat, kimyon, sumak falan; **2** Hayır, istemiyor. **3** Yarım kilo

Dialogue 4

1 Hayır; **2** Bilmiyorum. **3** dort

Dialogue 5

1 Bluz almak istiyor. **2** Bir bluz alıyor. **3** Evet

Language discovery

1 a Bugün ne yapıyoruz? **b** Ben istemiyorum. **c** Bir bluz bakıyorum. **d** Denemek istiyorum.

2 a -iyorum; **b** -iyor; **c** -ıyoruz; **d** -uyoruz; **e** -üyoruz

3 Dialogue 1: yapıyoruz?; bilmiyorum; istiyorum; Dialogue 3: istiyoruz; İstiyorsunuz? istiyor musunuz? istemiyorum; Dialogue 4: istiyoruz; diyoruz; yapıyoruz; geliyor; satıyoruz; yapıyoruz; yapıyorsunuz; koyuyoruz; satıyorsunuz? veriyoruz; Dialogue 5: bakıyorum; yakışmıyor; istiyorum; alıyorum; veriyorum; yapmıyoruz.

Practice

1 **a** 3; **b** 5; **c** 4; **d** 2; **e** 1

2 **1** e; **2** g; **3** a; **4** b; **5** f; **6** i; **7** h; **8** c; **9** d; **10** k; **11** j

3 **Food:** çerez; elma çay; lokum; fıstık; padişah macunu; incir; Türk kahvesi; bal; baharat **Clothes:** T-shirt; bluz; pantolon; ceket; ayakkabı. **Presents:** kilim; CD; kaset; çanta; halı; cüzdan

4 **Positive: a** yapıyor; **b** istiyor; **c** geliyor; **d** koyuyor; **e** okuyor; **f** yüzüyor; **g** yakışıyor; **h** deniyor **Negative: a** yapmıyor; **b** istemiyor; **c** gelmiyor; **d** koymuyor; **e** okumuyor; **f** yüzmüyor; **g** yakışmıyor; **h** denemiyor

5 bikini; şort; güneş gözlüğü; güneş kremi; parmak arası; sandalet; bluz; ceket; şapka; pasaport; bilet

Speaking

Siz: 1 Merhaba. Deri ceketler ne kadar. **2** Kırk beden. **3** Mavi. **4** Çok pahalı. **5** Tamam alıyorum.

Reading and writing

1 Susan is sitting at a table in a café overlooking the seaside. While she is drinking a glass of fruit juice she is watching the people on the beach and in the sea. Three children are buying ice cream on the beach. A couple are lying on the sand. The woman is wearing a bikini and sunhat and is reading a book. The man is wearing shorts and sunglasses and is looking towards the sea. In the sea there is one rowing boat and one sailing boat. Seven people are swimming in the sea.

2 Answers will vary.

Test yourself

1 40 beden mavi bir ceket istiyorum, lütfen. **2** Naneli lokum, lütfen. **3** Yarım kilo kuru yemiş, lütfen. **4** Bir paket kimyon, lütfen. **5** Şarap içmiyorum.

UNIT 9

Cinema and theatre

1 at film festivals; **2** A hamam is a Turkish bath.

Vocabulary builder

A: Ne oynuyor? **B:** Bakalım. Galiba Hep Aşk Vardı oynuyor.

Dialogue 1

1 Sinemaya veya tiyatroya gitmek. **2** Kenterler'e gitmeye karar veriyorlar. (They decide to go to the Kenters'.)

Dialogue 2

1 Bilet ayırtmak istiyor; **2** İki bilet; **3** Kartla ödüyor

Dialogue 3

1 Hamam'ı görmeye karar veriyorlar. (They decide to see Hamam.)

2 Otobüsle

Dialogue 4

1 Gidiş-dönüş. 2 Dört bilet dört lira.

Language discovery

1 a Hafta sonunda ne yapalım? b Saat kaç? c Tamam hadi şimdi çıkalım.
d Hadi otobüsle gidelim.

3 a 5; b 6; c 3; d 2; e 1; f 4

5 a Tiyatroya...? b Hadi arayalım.

6 Dolmuşla ... otobüsle mi...?

Practice

1 alışveriş yapmak (to go shopping); sinemaya gitmek (to go to the cinema); tiyatroya gitmek (to go to the theatre); restorana gitmek (to go to a restaurant); müzeye gitmek (to go to the museum); televizyon seyretmek (to watch TV); müzik dinlemek (to listen to music); yüzmek (to swim); seyahat etmek (to travel)

    a   tiyatroya gitmek; sinemaya gitmek; restorana gitmek; televizyon seyretmek

    b   Televizyon seyretmeye karar verdiler. (They decided to watch TV.)

    c   **Yeşim** Bu akşam ne yapalım?

Ahmet	Tiyatroya gidelim.
Yeşim	Çok pahalı.
Ahmet	Sinemaya gidelim mi?
Yeşim	Sinemalar çok uzak.
Ahmet	Restorana gidelim.
Yeşim	Ben rejimdeyim.
Ahmet	Ne yapalım?
Yeşim	Televizyon seyredelim mi?
Ahmet	Çok iyi fikir. Gazeteye bakalım neler var.

2 4 ağustos Pazartesi akşam 8'de Banu'yla tiyatroya gidiyorum; 5 ağustos salı serbestim/boşum; 6 ağustos perşembe bir buçukta Gonca ile yemeği yiyoruz; 7 ağustos perşembe serbestim/boşum; 8 ağustos cuma günü Yeşim ve Ahmet ile Boğaz gezisi yapıyoruz; 9 ağustos cumartesi günü saat ikide Çemberlitaş Hamamı'na gidiyorum; 10 ağustos pazar günü Vanesa ile Karagöz ve Hacivat'a gidiyoruz

3 a on iki otuz; yarım; b on beş on beş; üçü çeyrek geçiyor; c sekiz elli; dokuza on var; d dört yirmi beş; dördü yirmi beş geçiyor; e onsekiz kırk beş; yediye çeyrek var

4 a İkiyi beş geçiyor. **b** Üçe yirmi beş kala. **c** Dördü çeyrek geçe. **d** Yediye çeyrek var. **e** Yarımda.

5 a sinemada; **b** tiyatroda; **c** İşte; **d** parkta; **e** otobüste; **f** trende; **g** vapurda; **h** dolmuşta; **i** uçakta; **j** durakta; **k** otelde

6 a 3; 1; 2; 4; **b** 4; 2; 1; 3 or 4; **c** 4; 3; 2; 1

7 a 3 or 4; **b** 5; **c** 2; **d** 4 or 3; **e** 1

Reading and writing

Reading a timetable

1 from Eminönü; 2 three boats: at 10.35, 12.00 and 13.35; 3 At seven places; the seventh place is the last stop. 4 for three to five hours

Reading a message

Let's love nature and protect the forests.

Speaking

Sen: Hadi paba gidelim. Televizyon seyredelim mi? Çok iyi fikir. Hadi.

Test yourself

1 Tiyatroya gidelim mi? İyi bir oyun var. **2** İstanbul'a iki gidiş-dönüş bileti lütfen. **3** üçü çeyrek geçiyor; **4** Saat kaç? **5** Bu pazar için bir bilet lütfen.

UNIT 10

Atatürk, Mustafa Kemal

1 He is the founder of the Turkish Republic. **2** He won the wars against the occupying powers; he made Turkey an autonomous state in 1923. Then he started his cultural reforms to westernise, democratise and secularise Turkey, and he succeeded.

Vocabulary builder

Harikaydı. Ah, yemekler harikaydı.

Past time expressions: dün akşam; dün gece; geçen hafta sonu; geçen ay

Dialogue 1

1 Harikaydı. (It was wonderful.) **2** Her gün yüzdüler; sandalda kürek çektiler; kumlarda yürüdüler. **3** Harikaydı.

Dialogue 2

1 Berbattı. (It was terrible.); **2** Önce çok sıcaktı; sonra rüzgarlı ve yağmurluydu. **3** Hayır, sevmedi. Çünkü gürültülüydü, inşaat manzarayı kapatıyordu (manzara yoktu), müzik çok gürültülüydü yatak sertti ve duş bozuktu. **4** Berbattı, lezzetsizdi. Her şey çok pahalıydı.

Language discovery

1 a Harikaydı. **b** Tatil ve yemekler; **c** Önce çok sıcaktı, sonra rüzgarlı ve yağmurluydu. **d** Yemekler berbattı.

3 Happy holidaymaker: **a** 1; **b** 2; **c** 8; **d** 4; **e** 9; Unhappy holidaymaker: **a** 3; **b** 2; **c** 10; **d** 7; **e** 5

4 **a** -dı; **b** -ydı; **c** -ydı; **d** -tı; **e** -ti

Practice

b bin dört yüz elli üç; **c** 1920; **d** bin dokuz yüz otuz beş; **e** 1977; **f** iki bin on dört

Listening

1 Elvis Presley; **2** Evet; yaptı. (Yes, he did.) **3** Priscilla Beaulieu ile evlendi. (He married Priscilla Beaulieu.) **4** Evet, çok yakışıklıydı. (Yes, he was.) **5** Müzisyendi. (He was a musician.) **6** Evet, çok ünlüydü. (Yes, he was.) **7** Evet, dinledim/dinlemedim. (Yes, I did./No, I didn't.)

Speaking

Siz: – Plaja gittim. – Burda hava ve deniz çok güzeldi. Sen ne yaptın?

Reading

(possible answers) **1** Sultan Mehmet conquered Constantinople in 1453 and made it the capital of the Ottoman Empire. **2** The Ottomans built beautiful mosques, bridges and inns in Europe and Anatolia. **3** Atatürk won the War of Independence. Turkey became a republic, and Ankara became the capital city. Atatürk became the first president of the Republic and he carried out many reforms.

The Turks came to Anatolia from Central Asia. In 1071, Selçuk Turks came from Manzikert in the East to Anatolia and spread to the West. Osman Bey came as far as Bursa which then became the capital. In 1453, Sultan Mehmet the Conqueror conquered Constantinople, making it the capital of the Ottomans. The Ottomans stopped in Vienna in central Europe. In Europe and Anatolia, the Ottomans built beautiful mosques, bridges and inns with large courtyards. After the First World War, the English, French, Italians and Greeks occupied Turkey. Atatürk won the War of Independence. Turkey became a republic. Ankara became the capital. Atatürk became the first president (the head of the republic) and made many reforms.

Writing

1 **a** Hayır, henüz içmedi. **b** Hayır, İstanul'da. **c** Hayır, henüz gezmedi.
2 Answers will vary.

Test yourself

1 Happy holidaymaker: **a** 1; **b** 2; **c** 6; **d** 7; **e** 9; Unhappy holidaymaker: **a** 10; **b** 8; **c** 5; **d** 4; **e** 3

2 **a** 2; **b** 4; **c** 3; **d** 1

3

b anlaşmak	anlaştım	anlaştın
c TV'ye çıkmak	TV'ye çıktım	TV'ye çıktın
d plak yapmak	plak yaptım	plak yaptın
e evlenmek	evlendim	evlendin
f boşanmak	boşandım	boşandın
g konser vermek	konser verdim	konser verdin
h oynamak	oynadım	oynadın
i ödül almak	ödül aldım	ödül aldın
j ölmek	öldüm	öldün

4 **a** 8; **b** 10; **c** 1; **d** 9; **e** 2; **f** 3; **g** 4; **h** 5; **i** 6; **j** 7

5 **1** geldi(ler); **2** girdi(ler); **3** yayıldı(lar); **4** geldi; **5** oldu; **6** aldı; **7** yaptı; **8** durdu (lar); **9** yaptı(lar); **10** etti(ler); **11** kazandı; **12** oldu; **13** oldu; **14** oldu; **15** yaptı.

6 **a** Hiç tavla oynadın mı? **b** Hiç nargile içtin mi? **c** Hiç simit yedin mi? **d** Hiç deveye bindin mi? **e** Hiç çamur banyosu yaptın mı? **f** Hiç Ayasofya'yı gezdin mi? **g** Hiç hamama gittin mi? **h** Karagöz ve Hacivat'ı seyrettin mi?

7 **b** Salı yağmurluydu. **c** Çarşamba rüzgarlıydı. **d** Perşembe ılıktı. **e** Cuma bulutluydu. **f** Cumartesi serindi./or soğuktu. **g** Pazar sıcaktı.

8 (Possible answers) **a** Evdeydim. **b** Televizyon seyrettim. **c** Hayır, evde değildim. **d** Parka gittim. **e** Evet, seyrettim./Hayır, seyretmedim. **f** Evet, gittim./Hayır, gitmedim. **g** Evet, gezdim./Hayır, gezmedim. **h** Evet, dinledim./Hayır dinlemedim.

9 **a** Tatilin/tatiliniz nasıldı? **b** Berbattı. Her şey çok kötüydü. **c** Hamama gittim. **d** Çamur banyosu yapmadım. **e** Hiç deveye bindin mi?

Turkish–English glossary

AB	*EU*
ABD	*USA*
abi	*elder brother*
abla	*elder sister*
acaba	*I wonder/please*
acıkmak	*to get hungry*
acıktım	*I'm hungry*
açık	*open/light* (colour)
açmak	*to open/to switch on*
ad	*name*
ada	*island*
adres	*address*
adım	*my name* (first name)
adınız	*your name*
afedersiniz	*excuse me*
afiyet olsun	*enjoy your drinks!/enjoy your meal!*
ağır	*heavy*
ağrımak	*to ache*
ağrıyor	*aching*
ağustos	*August*
Akdeniz	*Mediterranean*
akıl	*intelligence*
akıllı	*clever, intelligent*
akılsız	*stupid, silly*
akşam	*evening*
akşamlar	*evenings*
aktör	*actor*
aldı	*conquered, took*
alfabe	*alphabet*
alışveriş	*shopping*
almak	*to buy/to take*
Alman	*German* (people)
Almanca	*German* (language)
Almanya	*Germany*
alo	*hello* (on the phone)
altın	*gold*

ama	*but*
amca	*uncle*
Amerika	*America*
Amerikalı	*American* (people)
Anadolu	*Anatolia*
anahtar	*key*
anlamak	*to understand*
anlaşmak	*to sign a contract*
anne	*mother*
annemler	*my parents* (lit. *my mothers*)
antika	*antique*
apartman	*apartment, flat*
ara sıra	*sometimes*
araba	*car*
aralık	*December*
aramak	*to call*
arası	*between*
arasında	*in between*
arayayım	*let me call/I'll call*
arkadaş	*friend*
arkadaşım	*my friend*
arı	*bee*
arı soktu *a*	*a bee has stung me*
arslan sütü	*raki* (lit. *lion's milk*)
askerliğini yaptı	*did his military service*
askerlik	*military service*
aspirin	*aspirin*
Asya	*Asia*
Asyalı	*Asian*
atmak	*to put*
Avrupa	*Europe*
Avrupalı	*European*
Avustralya	*Australia*
Avustralyalı	*Australian*
ayakkabı	*shoes*
ayakkabıcı	*shoe shop*
Ayasofya	*St Sophia*
ayırtmak	*to book, to reserve*
ayran	*yogurt-based drink*
ayrı	*separate*
baba	*father*
baharat	*spices*
bahşiş	*tip*

bakalım	*let's have a look*
bakkal	*grocer/grocer's*
baklava	*baklava* (Turkish dessert)
bakmak	*to look*
bal	*honey*
balık	*fish*
balıkçı	*fishing/fisherman*
balkon	*balcony*
balkonlu	*with a balcony*
bana	*me, for me*
bana da	*for me too*
bana Yasemin deyin	*call me Yasemin*
banka	*bank*
banknot	*banknotes*
banyo	*bathroom*
barbunya	*red mullet*
bardak	*glass*
basketbol	*basketball*
baş	*head*
Başbakan	*Prime Minister*
başım ağrıyor	*I have a headache*
başka	*what else*
başka bir şey	*anything else*
başkent	*capital*
bayanlar	*ladies*
baylar	*gentlemen*
bayram	*celebration*
bekar	*single*
Belçika	*Belgium*
Belçikalı	*Belgian* (people)
ben	*I*
ben de	*me too, I too*
bence	*in my opinion*
benden	*on me*
benim	*my, it's me*
benim için	*for me*
berbat	*terrible*
bey	*Mr* (after first names only)
beyefendi	*sir*
beyaz	*white*
beyaz peynir	*white cheese*
beyazlı	*dressed in white*
bıçak	*knife*

bırak!	leave!
bırakmak	to leave
biber	pepper
bikini	bikini
bile	even
bilet	ticket
bilet gişesi	ticket office
bilgisayar	computer
biliyor	he/she knows
biliyorum	I know
bilmek	to know
bilmiyorum	I don't know
bina	building
bir buçukta	at half past one
bira	beer
biraz	a little
birbirimiz	each other
birinci	first
Birinci Dünya Savaşı	First World War
bitkisel	herbal
biz	we
bluz	blouse
boş	vacant/empty
boşanmak	to get divorced
bozmak	to break
bozuk	change (money)/broken, out of order
bölge	region
börek	pastry
börekçi	pastry shop
Britanya	Britain
bu	this
buçuk	it's half past
buçukta	it's (at) half past
buğulama	steamed
bugün	today
Bulgar	Bulgarian (people)
Bulgarca	Bulgarian (language)
Bulgaristan	Bulgaria
bunlar	these are
burada	here
burası	here, this place
buraya	here (shows movement)
Bursa'ya kadar	as far as Bursa

butik	boutique
buyrun yes,	I'm listening to you/here you are/do come in
buyrun, efendim?	how can I help you, sir/madam?
büfe	food stall
büro	office
bütün	all
büyük	big, great
Büyük Britanya	Great Britain
cadde	street
cami	mosque
canım	my dear
canlı	alive, live
ceket	jacket
cevap	answer
cevap vermek	to answer
cezve	Turkish coffee maker
cızbız	sizzling/fried
ciddi	serious
cuma	Friday
cumartesi	Saturday
cumhurbaşkanı	president
cumhuriyet	republic
cüzdan	wallet, purse
çadır	tent
çalmak	to ring
çalışkan	hard-working
çamur	mud
çamur banyosu	mud bath
çanta	bag
çarşamba	Wednesday
çatal	fork
çay	tea
çek	pull
çekmek	to pull
çerez	snacks
çeşit	kind, type
çeşitli	various
çeyrek	a quarter
çık!	come out!/get out!
çıkmak	to come out/go up
çiçek	flower
çift	a pair
çikolatalı	chocolate flavoured/with chocolate

çizme	boots
çoban salatası	mixed salad
çocuk	child
çocuklar	children
çok	very
da	also
dağ	mountain
daha	more (adjective + -er)
dahil	included
dahil mi?	is it included?
dakika	minutes
dalgalı	rough
dalmak	to dive
-dan, (-den) sonra	after
danışma	information
dans	dance
dantel	lace
-de	at, on, in
dede	grandfather
değil	not
değil mi?	isn't it?
değişik	different
demokrasi	democracy
demokratik	democratic
-den beri	since
-den -e kadar	from ... to ...
-den önce	before
-den sonra	after
denemek	to try on
deniz	sea
deniz kenarları	seaside
deri	leather
ders	lesson, class
dersten sonra	after the class
devamlı	continuous
deve	camel
devrimler	reforms
dikkat et!	watch out!, pay attention!, be careful!
dil	language/tongue
dilimlenmiş	sliced
doğmak	to be born
doğru	right/true/straight
doğum tarihi	date of birth

doğum yeri	*place of birth*
doktor	*doctor*
dolmuş	*sharing taxi*
dolmuşla	*by sharing taxi*
domates	*tomatoes*
don	*frost*
dondurma	*ice cream*
dön	*turn!*
döner	*doner*
dönmek	*to turn/return/rotate* (takes **-e** or **-a** ending, e.g., **sola dön**)
dönüş	*return*
durak	*stop, bus stop*
durdular	*stopped*
durmak	*to stop*
duş	*shower*
dut	*mulberry*
dün	*yesterday*
dünya	*world*
dürüst	*honest*
düz	*straight*
-e, -a kadar	*as far as*
eczane	*chemist's*
efendim	*sir or madam/pardon*
efendim?	*pardon?*
Ege	*Aegean*
eğlence	*entertainment*
ekim	*October*
ekmek	*bread*
elbise	*dress*
eldiven	*gloves*
elektrik	*electricity*
elma	*apple*
elma çay	*apple tea*
emekli	*retired*
en	*the most* (*the* + adjective + *-est*)
en sıcak	*hottest*
en yakın	*nearest*
erkek	*man*
eski	*old*
esmer	*dark/olive skinned*
eşim	*my wife/my husband*
eşya	*goods*
et	*meat*

etek	skirt
etli	with meat
etsiz	without meat
ev	house, home
eve	to the house
evet	yes
evlenmek	to get married to
evli	married
eylül	September
fal bakmak	to read fortunes
falan	roughly, or so/and such like
farklı	different
farklıyız	we are different
Fatih Sultan Mehmet	Sultan Mehmet the Conqueror
festival	festival
fındık	hazelnuts
fırın	bakery/oven
fıstık	nuts
fıstıklı	nutty
fikir	idea
film	film
fiyatlar	prices
Fransa	France
Fransız	French (people)
Fransızca	French (language)
futbol	football
Galce	Welsh (language)
Galler	Wales
Galli	Welsh (people)
galiba	I think
garson	waiter/waitress
gazete	newspaper
gece	night
gece yarısı	midnight
geç	cross!/late
geç kaldım	I'm late
geçen	last
geçiyor (-i)	past
geçmek	to cross
geldim	I've come/I came
gelecek	next, coming
gelmek	to come
genel telefon	public phone

genellikle	*generally*
gerçekten	*really*
gerek	*necessary*
gezi	*trip/journey*
gezmek	*travel/trip*
gidelim mi?	*shall we go?*
gidin	*go (please)*
gir	*enter!*
girdi	*entered*
giriş	*entrance*
girmek	*to enter*
gişe	*ticket office*
git	*go!*
gitmek	*to go*
giysi	*clothes*
gökkuşağı	*rainbow*
gölge	*shade*
gömlek	*shirt*
görmek (-i)	*to see*
görüşmek(ile)	*to see each other*
görüşürüz	*see you*
gözlük	*glasses*
gramlık	*per gram*
gri	*grey*
gül	*rose*
güle güle	*goodbye (reply to hoşça kal or hoşça kalın)*
güle güle kullanın!	*enjoy using it*
gümrük	*customs*
gün	*day*
gün batımı	*sunset*
güneş	*sun*
güneşli	*sunny*
güney	*south*
günlük	*daily*
gürültü	*noise*
gürültülüydü	*it was noisy*
güzel	*beautiful, nice*
hadi	*let's/come on*
hadi, arayalım	*let's call*
hafta	*week*
hafta sonu	*weekend*
haklısınız	*you are right*
halı	*carpet*

hamam	Turkish bath (*Hamam* is also the name of a Turkish film)
hangi?	which?
Hanım	Miss/Mrs/Ms (after first names only)
Hanımefendi	lady, madam
harabe	ruin
harem	harem
harika	wonderful
harikaydı	it was wonderful
harita	map
hastahane	hospital
hava	air/weather
havaalanı	airport
havlu	towel
hayır	no
haziran	June
hediye	present
hediyelik şeyler	things for presents
hem ... hem	both ... and
hemen	straight away
henüz	only, yet
hep	all
hepsi bu kadar	that's all
her	every
her gün	everyday
her zaman	always
her şey	everything
her şey her şey	absolutely everything
hesap	the bill
hızlı	fast
hiç	(not) at all, never
Hindistan	India
Hintçe	Hindi
Hintli	Indian (person)
hisar	fortress
hostes	flight attendant
hoş	nice, pleasant
hoş bulduk	the standard reply to *hoş geldiniz* or *hoş geldin*
hoş geldiniz	welcome
hoşça kalın	goodbye
ılık	warm
ılıktı	it was warm
ışıklar	lights

ızgara	grilled
içecek	drink
içecekleriniz	your drinks
içmek	to drink
ideal	ideal
iken	while/when
iklim	climate
ilginç	interesting
ilk	first
ilkbahar	spring
ilk yardım	first-aid post
incir	fig
İngiliz	English (people)
İngilizce	English (language)
İngiltere	England
insan	person
inşaat	building site
internet	internet
İrlanda	Ireland
İrlandaca	Irish (language)
İrlandalı	Irish (people)
iskele	port
İskoç	Scottish (people)
İskoçya	Scotland
İskoçyalı	Scottish (people)
İspanya	Spain
İspanyol	Spanish (people)
İspanyolca	Spanish (language)
istasyon	station
istemek	to want
istiyorum	I want/I would like
iş	work, job
işaret	sign
işgal etmek	to occupy
işgal ettiler	occupied
işsiz	unemployed
işte	here, here it is, there
it	push
İtalyan	Italian (people)
İtalyanca	Italian (language)
itmek	to push
iyi	good
iyi akşamlar	good evening

iyi geceler	*good night*
iyiyim	*I am fine*
iyiyiz	*we are well*
Japon	*Japanese* (people)
Japonca	*Japanese* (language)
Japonya	*Japan*
jimnastik salonu	*gym*
kabak	*courgette/pumpkin*
kaç beden?	*what size?*
kaç gün?	*how many days?*
kaç günlük?	*for how many days?*
kaç kişi?	*how many people?*
kaç kişilik?	*for how many people?*
kaç lira?	*how much?, how many lira?*
kaç saat?	*how many hours?*
kadın	*woman*
kahvaltı	*breakfast*
kahvaltıda	*at breakfast*
kahve(ler)	*coffee(s)*
kahveli	*coffee flavoured*
kahverengi	*brown*
kalacak yer listesi	*lists of accommodation*
kalkan	*turbot*
kalkış	*leaving*
kalkmak	*to get up, to leave*
kalmak	*to stay*
kamp	*campsite*
Kanada	*Canada*
Kanadalı	*Canadian* (people)
Kapalı Çarşı	*Grand Bazaar*
kapatmak	*to close/to switch off/to cover*
kar	*snow*
Karadeniz	*the Black Sea*
kardeş	*sibling*
kardeşim	*my sister/my brother*
karışık	*mixed*
karışık meyve	*mixed fruit*
karpuz	*watermelon*
karşı	*opposite*
kart	*card*
kartla	*by card* (see **ile**)
kaset	*tape*
kasım	*November*

kayısı	apricot
kazak	jumper
kazandı	won
kazanmak	to win
kemer	belt
kere	times
kervansaraylar	inns with large courtyards
keyif	pleasure, delight, joy, enjoyment
keyifli	joyous, pleasurable, enjoyable
kez	time
KDV	VAT
Kıbrıs	Cyprus
Kıbrıslı	Cypriot
kır	countryside/wild
kır çiçekleri	wild flowers
kırmızı	red
kış	winter
kızarmış	toasted
kızımız	our daughter
kilim	woven rug
kilise	church
kilo	kilo
kiloluk	for a kilo
kimyon	cumin
kiralık	for rent
kiremit	brick
kiremitte	baked/roasted on a tile in the oven
kişi	person
kolay	easy
komedi	comedy
komik	funny
konser	concert
kontrol	check-in
korku	horror
korumak	to protect
koymak	to put, to put on
köfte	Turkish meatballs
köfteci	restaurant serving Turkish meatballs
köftelik	for meatballs
köpek	dog
köprü	bridge
köşe	corner
kötü	bad

kötüydü	*it was bad*
köy	*village*
kral	*king*
kredi	*credit*
kredi kartı	*credit card*
krem rengi	*beige*
kuaför	*hairdresser*
kum	*sand*
kumlar	*sands*
kurak	*dry*
Kurban Bayramı	*the Feast of the Sacrifice, celebration*
Kurtuluş Savaşı	*War of Independence*
kuru yemiş	*dried fruit*
kutu	*box*
küçük	*small*
kültür	*culture*
kültürel	*cultural*
küpe	*earrings*
kürek çekmek	*to row a boat*
küvet	*bath*
lahmacun	*savoury pancake*
levrek	*bass*
lezzetli	*tasty*
likör	*liquor*
liman	*port*
limonata	*still lemonade*
limonlu	*lemon flavoured*
liste	*list*
lokanta	*restaurant*
lokum	*Turkish delight*
lokumcu	*Turkish delight shop*
lüfer	*blue fish*
lüks	*luxury*
lütfen	*please*
maalesef	*unfortunately* (a polite remark)
magazin	*magazine*
Malazgirt	*town in southeast Turkey*
manken	*model*
manzara	*view*
manzaralı	*with a view*
Marmara	*Marmara*
mart	*March*

masa	table
masada	on the table
masmavi	very intense blue
mavi	blue
Mavi Yolculuk	Blue Cruise
mayıs	May
mayo	swimming costume
memnun oldum	I'm glad
merhaba/selam	hello/hi
merkez	centre
mermer	marble
meslek	job, profession
meşgul	busy
meşgulüm	I am busy
meşgulüz	we are busy
metal rengi	metallic colour
mevsim	season
meydan	square
meyve	fruit
meyveli	fruit flavoured/with fruit
meze	starter
Mısır	Egypt
Mısırlı	Egyptian (people)
milliyet	nationality
modern	modern
mor	purple
mönü	menu
muhteşem	great
mutlu	happy
mutsuz	unhappy
mücevher	jewellery
mühendis	engineer
Müslüman	Muslim
müze	museum
müzik	music
müzikal	musical
nane	mint
naneli	peppermint flavoured
nargile	hookah
nasıl?	how?
nasıl yazılır?	how do you spell it?
nasılsın? (sen)	how are you?

nasılsınız? (siz)	*how are you?*
NATO	*NATO*
ne?	*what?*
ne oynuyor?	*what's on?*
ne yapalım?	*what shall we do?*
neden?	*why?*
neler?	*what are there?*
nerede?/nerde?	*where?*
nereler?	*what places?*
nerelisin?	*where are you from?*
neresi?	*where/which place?*
nereye?	*where to?* (shows movement)
nereye gidelim?	*where shall we go?*
Nescafé	*instant coffee*
neyle? (ne ile)	*by what?/with what?/how* (see **ile**)
niçin? (ne için)	*why?*
nisan	*April*
nişanlı	*engaged*
nişanlın	*your fiancé*
numara	*number*
o	*that* (referring to something relatively far away)
o	*he/she/it*
ocak	*January*
oda	*room*
ofis	*office*
okumak	*to read*
olarak	*as*
onlar	*they*
orada	*there*
orijinal	*original*
orman	*forest*
orta	*medium*
Orta Asya	*Central Asia*
Orta Avrupa	*Central Europe*
orta boy	*medium sized*
ortada	*in the middle/centre*
ortalama	*average*
oruç	*fast*
oruç tutmak	*to fast*
Osman Bey	*Osman* (the head of the Ottoman clan)
Osmanlılar	*Ottomans*
otel	*hotel*
otobüs	*bus*

otobüs bileti	bus ticket
otobüs durağı	bus stop
otobüsle	by bus
otoyol	motorway
oturmak	to sit
oynamak	to act, to play
oyun parkı	play area
ödemek	to pay
ödül	award
öğlen	noon
öğrenci	student
öğrenmek	to learn
öğretmek	to teach
öğretmen	teacher
ölmek	to die
önce	at first, ago
önümüzde	in front of us
özel	special
özellikle	especially
özür dilemek	to apologise
özür dilerim	I'm sorry
padişah	sultan
padişah macunu	aphrodisiacs
pahalı	expensive
paket	packet, parcel
pansiyon	guest house
pantolon	trousers
park	park
parti	party
pasaport	passport
pasaport numarası	passport number
pasta	cake
pastahane/pastane	cake shop
patates	potatoes
patlıcan	aubergine
pazar	Sunday/market, bazaar
pazarlık	bargain
pazarlık yapmak	to bargain/haggle
pazartesi	Monday
pembe	pink
pencere	window
perde	curtain
perşembe	Thursday

peynir	cheese
pide	Turkish pizza
pideci	Turkish pizza restaurant
pilav	cooked rice
pilavlı	with cooked rice
piliç	chicken
piyaz	white bean salad
plaj	beach
plak	record
platin	platinum
politik	political
popüler	popular
porsiyon	portion
portakal rengi	orange (colour)
posta	post
prodüksiyon	production
profesör	professor
program	programme
rafadan	soft-boiled egg
rahat	comfortable
rahatsız etmeyin!	do not disturb!
rakı	aniseed-flavoured spirit
Ramazan	Ramadan
reçel	jam
rejimdeyim	I'm on a diet
renk(ler)	colour(s)
resepsiyon memuru	receptionist
restoran	restaurant
rica ederim	not at all
roka	rocket leaves
Rus	Russian (people)
Rusça	Russian (language)
Rusya	Russia
rüya	dream
rüzgar	wind
rüzgarlı	windy
rüzgarsız	without wind, windless
saat	time, hour or clock
saat kaç?	what time is it?
saat kaçta?	at what time?
sabah	morning
saç	hair
sade	plain/vanilla flavour/without sugar

sağ	right
sağ olun/sağ ol	thanks (showing respect and gratitude)
sağda	on the right
sahil	coast
sakin	calm
salam	salami
salatalık	cucumber
salı	Tuesday
samimi	friendly
sana	for you, to you
sandal	rowing boat
sandalet	sandals
saniye	seconds
saray	palace
sarı	yellow
satmak	to sell
sebze	vegetables
sekreter	secretary
seküler	secular
Selçuk Türkleri	Seljuk Turks
sen	you (singular)
serin	cool
sert	hard
servis	service
sevgi	affection, love
sevgili	beloved, dear
seviyorlar	they love
seviyorum	I like
seviyoruz	we like/love
sevmek	to love
sevmiyoruz	we do not like/love
seyahat	travel
seyahat acentası	travel agency
seyretmek	watch
sıcak	hot
sıfır	zero
oo	sign for toilet
sıkıcı	boring
sıkılmak	to be bored
simit	bread (in the shape of a large ring)
sinema	cinema
sır	secret
sırrımız	our secret

sis	fog
sisli	foggy
siyah	black
siyah gözlü	dark-brown eyed (lit. black eyed)
siyah saçlı	black haired
siz/sen	you (see Unit 1)
sizin	your
sizin için	for you
sokmak	to sting
sol	left
sonbahar	autumn
sonra	than/later
sor	ask!
sormak	to ask
sosis	sausage
soyadı	surname
soyadım	my surname
sözlük	dictionary
spor	sport
su	water
sucuk	spicy Turkish sausage
sudan ucuz	very cheap
sumak	sumac
susadım	I'm thirsty
sür	drive
sürmek	to drive
süt	milk
sütlü	with milk
şafak	sunrise
şampuan	shampoo
şans	chance/luck
şapka	hat
şarap	wine
şarap rengi	wine-coloured
şarkıcı	singer
şeker	sugar
Şeker Bayramı	feast marking the breaking of the fast
şekerli	with sugar, sweet
şekersiz	without sugar
şemsiye	umbrella
şimdi	now
şiş kebap	shish kebab
şişe	bottle

şoför	driver
şu	that is/that
şubat	February
şunlar	these
şurada	there
şurası	there, that place
tabii	of course
takım elbise	suit
taksi	taxi
Taksim	Taksim Square (in Istanbul)
tam	right/exactly/adult/full price
tamam	OK
tarif	recipe
tarih	history/date
tarihi	ancient, historic
taşımak	to carry
tatil	holiday
tatiliniz	your holiday
tatiller	holidays
tatlı	dessert
tatlı yiyelim, tatlı konuşalım	let's eat sweet, speak sweet (a common saying when offering sweets)
tava	fried/frying pan
tavla	backgammon
taze	fresh
tek kişilik	single room
tek yataklı	single bed
tekrar	again
tekstil	textile
telefon numaraları	telephone numbers
tembel	lazy
temiz	clean
temizlik yapmak	to do the cleaning
temmuz	July
tenis	tennis
tereyağı	butter
teşekkür(ler)	thanks
teyze	maternal aunt
tık tık	knock knock
tiyatro	theatre
Topkapı Müzesi	Topkapi Museum
tost (peynirli tost)	toasted sandwich (toasted cheese sandwich)
tren	train

turist	tourist
turizm	tourism
tüm	all
turkuaz mavi	turquoise
turuncu	orange
tuvalet	toilet
tuz	salt
tür	kind
Türk	Turkish (people)
Türk kahvesi	Turkish coffee
Türkçe	Turkish (language)
Türkiye	Turkey
Türkler	Turks
TV'ye çıkmak	to be on TV
ucuz	cheap
uçak	aeroplane
uzak	far
uzun boylu	tall/long
uzundur	it is tall/long
ülke	country
üniversite	university
ünlü	famous
üstü kalsın	keep the change
üzüm	grapes
valiz	suitcase
vapur	boat
var	there is/are
varış	arrival, arriving
varmak (-e)	to arrive
ve	and
vermek	to give
veya	or
villa expensive	detached house set in a garden
vişne suyu	sour cherry juice
voleybol	volleyball
ya siz?/ya sen?	and you?
yaşındayım	I'm x years old
yağıyor	it's raining
yağmak	to rain
yağmur	rain
yağmurlu	rainy
yağmursuz	without rain
yakın	near

yakında	soon
yakışıklı	handsome
yakışmak	to suit
yalı	old wooden villa
yanlış	wrong/false
yapmak	to do
yararlı	good for you
yarım	half/half past twelve
yarın	tomorrow
yasak	forbidden
yasaktır	it is forbidden
yasaktır	forbidden
yaş	age/old
yaşlı	aged
yatak	bed/mattress
yavaş	slowly
yavrum	my child (shows affection)
yaya	pedestrian
yayılmak	to spread
yaz	summer
yemek yemek	to eat food
yer	place, seat
yerken	while eating
yeşil	green
Yeşil Ev	Green House
yok	there is none/we haven't got any
yol	road
yolcu	traveller
yolcu vapuru	passenger boat
yolculuk	journey
yolumu kaybettim	I'm lost
yorgun	tired
yorgunum	I'm tired
yoruldum	I'm tired
yumurta	egg
yüksek	high/loud
yürümek	to walk
yürüyerek	on foot
yüzmek	to swim
yüzme havuzu	swimming pool
yüzük	ring
yüzyıl	century

zaman	*time*
zengin	*rich*
zeytin	*olives*
zeytinyağlı	*cooked with olive oil*
ziyaret	*visit*

Appendix of vowel harmony

E-TYPE ENDINGS

For **e**-type endings, use this rule:

e	goes after	**e, i, ö, ü**
a	goes after	**a, ı, o, u**

The following are **e**-type endings:

-ler	plural
-de	*at, on, in*
-mek	*to* (infinitive)
-e	*to, for*
-den	*from*
-me	*not*
-ce	makes a language word from a nationality word (adj)
-elim	*let's*
-le	*by, with, using*

I-TYPE ENDINGS

For **i**-type endings, use this rule:

i	goes after	**e, i**
I	goes after	**a, ı**
ü	goes after	**ö, ü**
u	goes after	**o, u**

Here are some common **i**-type endings:

-mı?	question word
-ı	Turkish equivalent of *the*
-cı	denotes a person or an occupation

-dır	*is*: very formal usage
-lı	*with, containing, from*
-iyor	*-ing* (present tense)
-dı	past tense
-lık	*-ness*
-siz	*without*

Grammar index

"Global scale" of the Common European Framework of Reference for Languages: learning, teaching, assessment (CEFR)

Advanced	**CEFR LEVEL C2**	Can understand with ease virtually everything heard or read. Can summarise information from different spoken and written sources, reconstructing arguments and accounts in a coherent presentation. Can express him/herself spontaneously, very fluently and precisely, differentiating finer shades of meaning even in more complex situations.
	CEFR LEVEL C1	Can understand a wide range of demanding, longer texts, and recognise implicit meaning. Can express him/herself fluently and spontaneously without much obvious searching for expressions. Can use language flexibly and effectively for social, academic and professional purposes. Can produce clear, well-structured, detailed text on complex subjects, showing controlled use of organisational patterns, connectors and cohesive devices.
Intermediate	**CEFR LEVEL B2** (A Level)	Can understand the main ideas of complex text on both concrete and abstract topics, including technical discussions in his/her field of specialisation. Can interact with a degree of fluency and spontaneity that makes regular interaction with native speakers quite possible without strain for either party. Can produce clear, detailed text on a wide range of subjects and explain a viewpoint on a topical issue giving the advantages and disadvantages of various options.
	CEFR LEVEL B1 (Higher GCSE)	Can understand the main points of clear standard input on familiar matters regularly encountered in work, school, leisure, etc. Can deal with most situations likely to arise whilst travelling in an area where the language is spoken. Can produce simple connected text on topics which are familiar or of personal interest. Can describe experiences and events, dreams, hopes and ambitions and briefly give reasons and explanations for opinions and plans.
Beginner	**CEFR LEVEL A2:** (Foundation GCSE)	Can understand sentences and frequently used expressions related to areas of most immediate relevance (e.g. very basic personal and family information, shopping, local geography, employment). Can communicate in simple and routine tasks requiring a simple and direct exchange of information on familiar and routine matters. Can describe in simple terms aspects of his/her background, immediate environment and matters in areas of immediate need.
	CEFR LEVEL A1	Can understand and use familiar everyday expressions and very basic phrases aimed at the satisfaction of needs of a concrete type. Can introduce him/herself and others and can ask and answer questions about personal details such as where he/she lives, people he/she knows and things he/she has. Can interact in a simple way provided the other person talks slowly and clearly and is prepared to help.

© Council of Europe. www.coe.int/lang.

Extract reproduced with the permission of the Council of Europe, Strasbourg